Five Families

and

Eight Young Men

(Nashville and her Jewry 1850-1861)

BY FEDORA S. FRANK

PUBLISHED BY
TENNESSEE BOOK COMPANY
NASHVILLE, TENNESSEE

Dedicated to my Parents

Louis and Rosa Small

Preface

AMERICAN JEWISH HISTORY is fascinating, and, fortunately, it is possible to write it on this soil. Great masses of source materials are available, for—unlike the case in much of Europe—the few wars that have plagued us have barely touched the archival records.

American Jewry—an integral part of the larger America—is worth writing about. The United States has become a land of destiny, and intelligent Americans have responded by developing a sense of history. Just as our republic has come to power in the twentieth century, just as it has emerged to exercise world influence and to meet the challenge of its being, its Jewish community, too, has grown until today it may well be deemed the most generous, the most responsible body of its kind the world has yet known—no small achievement.

This book by Fedora S. Frank is an attempt to understand the American Jewish community by understanding the beginnings of American Jewish life in one locality, a Southern city distinguished for its stability, its dignity, its leadership, and its sense of *noblesse oblige*. If Nashville is the Athens of the South, its Jewish citizens have helped to make it so. The period under study here, however, is the period of Nashville Jewry's first decades of communal existence. The effort to recreate this history is particularly to be praised in view of the unfortunate fact that no congregational records, as such, have survived to document the course of this antebellum group.

The 1840's, the 1850's, and the early 1860's were notable years in the life of the Jews of this land. By that time they had already established themselves in every town and city of importance. They had struck root even on the wide stretches of the prairies and on the sad wastes of the unending plains. Undaunted, the boldest and the daring, coming around the Horn,

7

had ventured even into the little village of Yerba Buena, soon to become the proud city of San Francisco. They were an interesting breed of men, immigrants—most of them Germans—men of restless, pioneering spirit who had the ambition, the will, and the native intelligence to hew out an existence for themselves. They had confidence in this land—and in themselves.

Though frequently of little distinction and of less success, these many thousands, in their own quiet and unassuming manner, appear to us, their children, to be cast in a heroic mold. With their packs on their backs, they moved into the villages and onto the farmsteads of the ever-receding frontier, where they dedicated themselves to the rearing of their own families and to the strengthening of their age-old faith.

It was in those days that five families and eight young men came to Nashville to build a synagogue in that town. This is the story of how that Jewry grew, in devotion and in hope, to become what it is today. This is the story of its beginnings, of its social, cultural, religious, and economic life, painstakingly pieced together by a conscientious historian who has proven that the dead *can* rise again. How grateful we are to her for making these dry bones live. Let us but have a hundred honest monographs such as this, built on fact, on truth, on honest research, and, if need be, on harsh reality, and we shall yet have an American Jewish history worthy of the name.

Jacob R. Marcus

American Jewish Archives
Cincinnati, Ohio

Introduction

THE TITLE "Five Families and Eight Young Men" is taken from a letter written August 8, 1852 by Isaac Garritson of Nashville to the prominent and unofficial "Chief Rabbi" of America of that period, Isaac Leeser of Philadelphia. This letter is noteworthy as it is one of the oldest bits of factual information about the Jews of Nashville. Mr. Garritson wrote, "We have established here last year, a Hebrew Benevolent Society . . . it is at present very small yet numbering only 5 families and about 8 young men . . ."

Although I am indebted to Mr. Garritson for the title of this book, the story pertains to many more people. It is the saga of Nashville and her Jewry during the decade of the 1850's. This was truly a fabulous era in American life. It was a time of growth and expansion, of culture and enlightenment, of strife and secession. It was the decade that witnessed the permanent establishment of a Nashville Jewish Community. This portrait of Nashville attempts to picture life in Nashville as witnessed and experienced by this small group of courageous immigrants who left no records that tell us of their appalling difficulties or their rewarding successes. They speak to us from the yellowed pages of court proceedings, from the almost illegible records of the government census and from the enlightening advertisements of newspapers and periodicals. May this book be a tribute to the industry, self-reliance and memory of antebellum Nashvillians of all creeds.   Fedora S. Frank

Table of Contents

"To everything there is a season, and a time to every purpose under the heaven." Ecc. 3:1

List of Illustrations

(Pages 65 through 72)

CHAPTER I

A Time to be Born

THE TIME was the fabulous fifties, a decade of progress and enlightenment. Among the population of 10,165 persons[1] who celebrated Nashville's 70th anniversary in 1850 was a small nucleus of men who established the first permanent local Jewish community. For an explanation of the absence of Jews in early Nashville history let us turn our attention to the beginnings of American Jewry.

The story of the individual Jew in American history began in 1492 with the discovery of America. Among the crew of the Genoese sailor, Christopher Columbus, were five Jews,[2] and the legend goes that the first man to step on the soil of the New World was the Jewish interpreter of the group, Luis de Torres. However, it is to the twenty-three Dutch Jewish refugees fleeing Brazil following its seizure by Portugal that we owe the beginnings of American Jewry. This was 1654, and the port of entry was Niew Armsterdam now known as New York.

At the close of the Revolution, after more than a century of residence, there existed in all the Thirteen Colonies only about 2,500 Jews.[3] As their numbers were always small in proportion to the population, they did not scatter far from organized Jewish communities where congregations had been established.

Probably, the earliest story concerning the settlement of Jews in Tennessee was one concerning a visionary project of an early explorer of the Tennessee country, a Scottish Lawyer, Sir Alexander Cuming.[4] Inspired, so it is said, by a dream of his wife, Sir Alexander went to South Carolina in 1729 and got himself appointed chief and lawgiver of the Cherokee Indians. The following year he returned to England and presented seven of the Cherokee chiefs to the king. In 1748 Cuming proposed

15

to Lord Halifax as a revenue raising government scheme, the settlement of 300,000 Jewish families on the lands of the Cherokee Indians. The families were to be settled in the Cherokee Mountains "as industrious, honest subjects" to develop that promising but little known region. When the government refused consideration of the project, the prominent Jews of London gave Cuming hearings to consider the scheme. Finally Sir Alexander proposed to open a subscription of £500,000 to establish provincial banks in America for such a settlement. Needless to say nothing ever came of this fanciful dream.

Among the early traders and trappers who roamed the Tennessee country in the 18th century it is quite likely that a few Jews were to be found. An unauthenticated story[5] tells of a few Jewish settlers along the Holston River in East Tennessee as being the only settlement of Jews in the state before the 19th century.

An interesting but theoretical study based on the 1790 census of the surnames of the 31,913 people living in the territory that later became Tennessee estimated the nationalities of those residents as English, Irish, Scotch, Dutch, French, German, and stated that all others including Hebrews were thirty-two.[6]

Prior to the Revolution, Tennessee had been a part of the state of North Carolina. It was ceded to the Federal government in 1790 and became the Territory South of the Ohio until it was admitted into the Union in 1796 as the sixteenth state. The great majority of the early settlers were North Carolinians who found the Cumberland Gap an accessible gateway to the promising Western country. Furthermore, many North Carolinians had been given lands in reward for military service. As late as 1850 the census records revealed that 7.2% of the population of Tennessee had come from North Carolina. In an attempt to unearth the beginnings of Tennessee Jewry it is only natural that we turn our attention to the mother state. Were Jews among the early North Carolinians who settled in the new country? Colonial North Carolina did not attract many Jews to her borders. Although there was liberty of worship, the Church of England was the established state church, and law permitted only members of the church to hold office. There were few large cities, no markets, and opportunities were more attractive in the other colonies.[7] Both the colonial and state records contain many names that reflect Jewish beginnings. We read of the Israels, the Isaacs, Solomons, Moses, Mordecais but we can not positively establish that they were Jews. Two of the most ancient names in Jewish history designating the priestly caste are Cohen and Levi.[8] These two names having many variations in spelling were not unknown in several North Carolina counties in the 18th century.[9] An abstract of the will of Solomon Davis of Pasquatauk County mentions[10] a son-in-law, Cabb Coen, and a grandson, the son of Cabb, is called Daniel Koen signifying the change of name in one generation from Coen to Koen. One can only ponder the number of generations that were required to change the name of the probable progenitor Cohen to Coen. However, it is entirely possible that the name Coen was of Dutch origin.

We must not be misled by the presence of honored and cherished Jewish names in the North Carolina land grants or in early Davidson County deeds to property and marriage records. It is not to William Coen,[11] Aaron Cohen[12] also spelled Cohern, Henry, William, Thomas and James Levy[13] that we can trace the beginnings of middle Tennessee Jewry. These were probable descendants of a Jewish parent or grandparent who through intermarriage had left the ranks of their co-religionists. This drifting away from Judaism was quite common not only in colonial America but throughout the South in the 19th century. It would take years of study to give the full account of the many Southern families whose ancestors two or three generations ago were Jewish.[14] Who then were the early Jews? Can the cemeteries provide a few clues? The search in this direction was unrewarding. In traditional Jewish observances, the rites connected with death had real religious significance as they were associated with the hope of resurrection for a future life.[15] Early immigrants had a fear of dying alone; as soon as a few Jews settled in a community the first need to be met was the establishment of a cemetery. This the Jews of Nashville were able to do in 1851.[16] It is doubtful if more than one or two Jews were

17

ever buried in the city cemetery which had been opened with the sale of lots in 1820 and 1821. Earlier burials had been in an open land now known as Sulphur Dell. All lists of burials in the city cemetery prior to 1846 have been destroyed, and no official death records for the city or county were kept until 1874. So from the list that is available to us covering only the years 1846 to 1851 or 1852, the date of the establishment of the Jewish cemetery, two accounts merit our attention. One concerns the fees for the burial of one F. Fisher who died August 9, 1847, of inflammation of the brain.[17] A notation on the burial file stated that the fees were to be paid by Garrison. Undoubtedly this benefactor was Isaac Garritson, sometimes written Garrison and referred to in an early history of Davidson County as Isaac Gershon. Subsequent research reveals him to be the most prominent Nashville Jew of the 1840's and 1850's. The second item of interest is that one lot in the city cemetery was owned by Henry Harris, a son-in-law of Isaac Garritson.[18]

An examination of contemporary writings proves most conclusively that the Jew was not only a rarity but an unknown quantity in Nashville history prior to 1840. There is not a single reference to these people who in this era had the appellation of Hebrew or Israelite. The occasional Jew who might find himself in this sparsely settled area where there were no Jewish congregations would find it most difficult to observe his religion. As a result he tended to drift away from the faith into which he had been born and reared. Being young and unmarried he often became a victim of the inevitable loneliness which led to intermarriage. Another reason may be given for the presence of few known Jews in the first seventy years of Nashville history. Sometimes he concealed his identity. In many places he encountered distrust, was treated in an humiliating manner, as the picture of the Jew drawn by ecclesiastical hands did not inspire or encourage polite treatment;[19] and so, in the face of suspicion, distrust and contempt he was often forced to bury his origin.

An absorbing account of the homeless Jew who intermarried and then met ostracism and antagonism is revealed in the court records of the contested will of Jacob Rivers. On September

11, 1838, Jacob Rivers made a will leaving to his wife, his daughter and her heirs all his property. In November 1849, Rivers changed his will, making his niece his sole heir. After River's death in 1850, the daughter contested the will, and the court awarded her all of her father's property as she was able to show that her father's knowledge and approval of her marriage to one A. Cline "a man outside her faith" had in later years turned to opposition and estrangement.[20]

The researcher digging into the past is often able to stumble upon a few clues in odd and unexpected places. The records of the oldest existing Jewish congregation in this country, Sherith Israel of New York, revealed the earliest known birth of a Jewish child in Nashville. Only fifteen years after the modest settlement of less than 300 people at Fort Nashborough, there was born on December 2, 1795, Sarah, daughter of Benjamin and Hannah Hays Myers, in Nashville, Tennessee.[21] The father, Benjamin Myers, born in Newport in 1755 was the son of a Hungarian interpreter known as Myer Benjamin and an Austrian mother known only as Sarah, daughter of Myer. The baby's mother, Hannah, was born in New York, April 15, 1768, the daughter of David Hays and Esther Etting. Both the Hays and Etting families were prominent in pre-Revolutionary America. What brought Benjamin and his family to this outpost of civilization[22] will never be answered but we do know that the stay was of short duration as records reveal that another child was born in Virginia[23] in 1796.

The narrative of the Jew in Nashville prior to 1850 is truly an unconnected and fragmentary account of transitory and unknown names appearing in court records, on deeds to property, in marriage records, in newspaper listings of letters held at the post-office and in newspaper advertisements. One can not always be certain that the suspect was Jewish and often the Anglicized name of a Jew could be easily overlooked. The ancestry and religion of Nashville's first dental surgeon, A. Shymanski,[24] who arrived in 1820, will ever remain a mystery. H. W. Abrams advertised in 1828 that he would open a school in Mr. McComb's house on College Street for instruction of both sexes in the elements of the English language, arithmetic, penmanship, and geography.[25] Letters, held for Z. Rosendrah and Mr. Zadock at the postoffice in 1841, suggest a short term stay in this area.[26] Andrew Smolniker, an Austrian, born in 1795, came to America in 1837, but seemed to never stay long in one place. He received his citizenship in Davidson County Circuit Court in 1848.[27] An application for citizenship was made by a Mr. Lenz at the September 1839[28] term of the circuit court, but Mr. Lenz had departed before he could receive his final papers. Bernard Wallman wrote his name into the annals of the Criminal Court with the information he had been born in Hanover in 1820, had arrived in New Orleans in 1844, and in 1848 he announced his intentions of becoming a citizen.[29]

More information is available on Simon Pollock, an Austrian, who came to New York in 1837 and there made application for citizenship. In February 1843, he was given his final papers by the circuit court of Davidson County.[30] The necessary term of residence for the issuance of these second papers established his arrival in Nashville about 1840. Pollock was a doctor and in the local papers of the early 1840's he advertised himself as a "practitioner in medicine, surgery and obstetrics."[31]

It will never be known if it was poor business or the lure of California gold fields that shortened the Nashville residence of Dr. H. Fischel, a dentist, who advertised in Nashville newspapers that he "was prepared at all times to perform every branch of his profession in the best manner and on the most reasonable terms. Teeth plugged, drawn at all hours—artificial teeth from one to a whole set inserted on plate, also pivot which will be warranted to answer all purposes of articulation and mastication the same as nature itself."[32] Dr. Fischel also announced that he used a pain destroying agent known as chloroform. A year later on April 3, 1849, the *Nashville Gazette* published a letter it had received from Fischel which told of his experiences enroute to the gold diggings in California. Dr. Fischel wrote, "only nineteen days from Mexico we were beset by robbers and thieves . . . the stagecoaches are robbed daily . . . we expect to arrive in California about May 1."

For the brief period of six months beginning in the fall of 1849 and ending in March 1850, a local paper advertised the merits of a clothing renovator, one E. J. Lyons. Mr. Lyons referred to himself as a "wandering Jew" from Richmond, Virginia, who did no work on Saturdays.[33] He announced his ability to "remove stains and spots from silks and woolens caused by paint, oil, wax, turpentine or grease." His renovating liquid was for sale at his establishment on Market Street where he also whitened straw, leghorn and panama hats. It is possible that E. J. was Ellis Judah Lyons, a brother of Jacques Judah Lyons the well known Reader or *Hazzan* of the Spanish Portuguese Synagogue, Shearith Israel, of New York.[34] E. J. was born in Paramaribo, Surinam, Dutch Guiana, July 1811. His mother had been Mary Asser Levy of Philadelphia who had gone with the father, Judah Eleazer Lyons to South America after their marriage. E. J. came to America shortly after his marriage, and for a short time he too was the Reader or *Hazzan* of the Richmond, Virginia Synagogue. Here in 1847 he also conducted a school for "young ladies and gentlemen." A curriculum of "arithmetic, geography, astronomy, grammar, composition, philosophy, history and mythology was comparable to the liberal and classical education offered in the best seminaries."[35] E. J. was no mercenary educator; he offered free instruction to children of indigent parents.

To the hundreds of thousands of Europeans fleeing political uprisings, religious persecutions and economic distress, America was a promised land. It was inevitable that Nashville, the capital and largest city in the state, an embryonic wholesale center, would attract many of these newcomers.

And such was the immigrant English family, the Franklands, who arrived in Nashville in 1845 after a residence of some years in New York. Their sojourn in Nashville continued until 1849 when the family departed for Memphis where they lived for many years, becoming an active and contributing force in communal and religious life. It is from the writings of one of the Frankland sons, Abraham Ephraim, that information of this period is available. He wrote, "The Nashville congregation grew out of a small group who formed a *minyan*[36] in 1848 at the

21

residence of Isaac Garritson on Summer Street. Henry Harris was the reader and those who participated were S. Martin, E. Wolfe, Henry Jessel, A. E. Frankland, Louis Hanf, Mike Powers, Judah Franklin, Dr. Jacob Mitchell, Henry Nathan, Abraham Schwab and Julius Ochs."[37] Frankland's narrative was written in 1889; all research today indicates that his memory after forty years was none too accurate with several names. S. Martin was probably S. Marks, and Henry Nathan was undoubtedly Sinai Nathan.

In some form or fashion the lives of these men were intermingled with the growth and accomplishments of Nashville in that momentous decade that preceded the Civil War, and so we begin the story of those immigrants who dared remain loyal and faithful to the religion of their fathers as they applied themselves diligently and patiently to the American way of life.

CHAPTER II

A Time to Cast Away

O N a memorable day in 1845 the two youthful and courageous Elsbach boys, David age 14 and Max age 16, bade farewell to their loved ones in their native village of Waldsdorf in Saxony.[1] They were casting aside familiar faces and traditional customs for a new life in a strange land among unknown people. Theirs is the absorbing story of all stout-hearted European Jewish immigrants who with determination, faith and hope entered America in the mid-nineteenth century. To the meager information available concerning Nashville immigrants, we must supply those known facts to recreate the story of this mass movement to the Promised Land.

Nashvillians of the twentieth century are prone to refer to themselves as a homogeneous group and as descendants of pioneer stock. Strange as it may now seem, in 1850 one out of every eleven persons was foreign born.[2] In the decade with which this book is concerned, 1850-1860, America experienced the greatest increase in immigration in relation to the existing population than at any other time in its history. Two million immigrants, mostly from the German states, flooded into this country, and the 50,000 Jews who were here in 1850 had grown to 150,000 by 1860.

The seventh and eighth census reports, the Nashville business directories beginning with 1853, the Davidson County court records and the advertisements in the many daily and weekly newspapers disclose the names of approximately one hundred sixty heads of families who have been definitely identified as of the Jewish faith and who were living for some part or all of the decade 1850-1860 in Nashville. Approximately fifty percent were from Germany, forty percent from Poland and the remainder from England, France, Holland, Austria and Russia.[3]

23

Less than six were native born. Many discrepancies in records of the countries of birth have been detected in this study. In some instances the designation of Poland is confusing. In the period with which this inquiry is concerned there was no self-governing country known as Poland, it having been divided in the eighteenth century between Prussia, Austria and Russia. Undoubtedly, many of the forty percent, who listed Poland as the country of birth, came from Prussia or Austria; and the large number who originated in the vicinity of Warsaw should have classified themselves as Russians, as this area was a part of Czarist Russia until it was returned to a recreated Poland at the end of World War I. The immigrants Alexander Klein and Nathan Cline listed both Poland and Warsaw as birthplaces.

The Jew in early nineteenth century Europe was in truth a second class citizen; all sorts of restrictions were enacted against him. Württemberg had adopted a law in 1828 prohibiting the sale or exchange of property by Jews unless it had been occupied or farmed by the owners for at least three years.[4] This and other restraints practically drove the Jews from Württemberg where a Jewish teacher reported in 1856 that forty percent of the Jews in his community had left.[5] The conscription for army service drove the young men from many of the German states. Recorded in the archives of Württemberg is the story that of 206 Jewish immigrants of 1848-1855, sixty-one percent were below the age of twenty.

An edict of 1813 in Bavaria limited the number of Jews in the professions and in many businesses.[6] The exclusion from trades and professions, reinforced by restrictions in marriage permits and the successive years of economic distresses, drove the Jewish masses to the land of opportunity. From such situations as existed in Bavaria fled the Flashman brothers, Phillip and Nathan, Z. Levy and his eight nephews, the Nassauer boys, Isaac Stein and the Sulzbacher brothers.[7]

In Russia, the anti-Jewish measures were colored by the hatred of Czar Nicholas I (1825-55) for the Jews and his persistent attempts to convert them to Christianity. They were drafted into the army not at age eighteen as were other subjects, but at twelve and were required to give twenty-five years of service reckoned from the eighteenth year. This measure was intended to remove the Jewish youth from the influence of his religion.[8] These discriminatory measures resulted in wholesale migration of the Jews particularly in the area that had once been Poland and where a very large Jewish population existed.

The world was witnessing a whole new concept of freedom which had been nourished and advanced by the American and French struggles for independence. A desire for freedom grew in the hearts of all liberty loving and down trodden Europeans. This hope manifested itself in unsuccessful political uprisings in various German states. Many of these advocates of democracy were forced to flee to America. Rabbi Bertram W. Korn in his book, *Eventful Years and Experiences*, has identified as Jewish only forty of these political refugees of the uprisings of 1848. Two mentioned by Rabbi Korn were to be part of the Nashville scene in the 1850's. One was Bertha Levy who was to marry Julius Ochs in Nashville on February 28, 1855. Bertha, when only 16, had been a student at Heidelberg University when a fellow student was executed for revolutionary activities. She was among a group who went to wipe up the blood from the street, and the authorities mistook her action as rebellious. Her family was notified to get her out of the country; so she was sent to her uncle in Natchez, Mississippi.[9]

Another forty-eighter, who was to visit Nashville in 1856 to render an important religious decision, was Rabbi Bernard Illowy. Illowy's participation in the uprisings had been limited to an address made to the revolutionary army as it passed through his home town on the way to Prague.[10] He realized that even this small participation would destroy any chance of securing a rabbinical position; so he too turned his thoughts and dreams to the golden America.

The German outbreaks of 1848 and 1849 placed the authorities in a dilemma. To detain thousands of political prisoners was an expense; to free them entailed loss of prestige and the probability of future revolts. Baden sought a way out by offering to send the rank and file at its own expense to America.

Only a dozen or more accepted, the rest preferring jail and martyrdom.[11]

However, in one parish in Baden, three hundred sixty-nine non-revolutionary inhabitants out of a population of two thousand nine hundred and nineteen indicated their desire to leave for America.[12] Was there a remote possibility that Louis Sohn or Cohn, a signer of the charter to the first Jewish Synagogue in Nashville and a native of Baden, had been one of those who so signified his willingness to leave?[13]

As if the discriminatory measures, the political uprisings and the economic distresses were not sufficient reasons, the exodus received added boosts from newspaper editorials and advertisements. Following anti-Jewish riots in Bohemia the papers had articles, "On to America." Leopold Kompert wrote, "The person who is capable of becoming free commits the greatest wrong if he does not . . . whoever seizes the initiative in becoming free serves and carries the torch for thousands of Jews."[14] A writer in the New York German weekly *Israels Herold* wrote March 24, 1849, "Hundreds of Bohemians immigrated this year. The second class cabins of the boat leaving April 15 are completely taken by Jews from Prague."

The European papers carried advertisements and notices that told of the fortunes to be made in America in every field and particularly through investments in real estate. What an incentive for the poverty stricken Jewish lad who could still dream and hope! The American papers listed the banks and agencies that would forward money to Europe.

Similarly, the gazetteers and guide books were selling America. There were numerous travel books published in the 30's, 40's and 50's which advised prospective travelers on schedules of ships, coaches and trains. Suggestions were offered for necessary provisions for the long journey. The constitutions of both the Federal and State governments were also explained to these future American citizens. Cities were described, and the opportunities in agriculture and business were explained. "There was room for everybody in America with talent."[15] An early book described Nashville as a city of wealth, elegant mansions, thriving business

26

and great educational opportunities.[16] Many state governments had inaugurated legislation to encourage immigration to their state but Tennessee evidenced no interest in a project that might tend to reduce the dominant Anglo-Saxon stock.[17]

There were some ninety-five travelers to the antebellum South who wrote of their observations and experiences.[18] Ten of these were Germans and it is within reason to conclude that some of our immigrants read or heard portions of their books. Letters received in Europe from relatives and friends in America impressed the readers with the opportunities to be found in this new land. The arrival of money was proof sufficient that it was truly flowing with milk and honey. It is entirely possible that letters and money from young Elias Franklin to his family in Wakrova encouraged his brother Jacob[19] to follow him to *Das Goldene Land.*

Immigration was further stimulated by those who profited from it. An agent of the Pennsylvania railroad sold tickets in Bremen in 1856.[20] Agencies from Havre, London and Liverpool were maintained in Germany to recruit immigrants, and thousands were taken across the English channel to London and Liverpool before proceeding to America. This routing to America via England was popular for many of the German, Polish and Russian Jews. Possessing little money or worldly goods, they frequently found it necessary to remain in England to accumulate the passage for America.[21] Many settled there, married and begot children before they were able to resume their American venture. England was a popular stopover for many of Nashville's early Jewish settlers. In order to avoid military service a young teen-ager, Harris Abrahams, left his native Poland in the early 1850's for Nashville where he had an older brother. His meager funds allowed him to get no further than England where he remained long enough to assimilate a working knowledge of the language.[22] In 1854 Sarah, and in 1855 Sophy, daughters of the Polish couple Lewis and Esther Fry, were born in London. But the couple had reached Nashville by 1858 for the birth of their third daughter, Flora. Simon and Rosa Heims had two small children when they left their native Prussia. Isaac, the

27

third child, was born in England in 1853. The first child of Robert and Frances Blum was born in England in 1849 as was the firstborn of H. and Harriett Jacobs in 1856. Native born adult English Jews in antebellum Nashville included the three Powers brothers, Michael, Lewis and Sam, Priscilla Lipshar, Sampson Laufer, Esther Lande, Elizabeth Isaaks Lyons and Phoebe or Vogele Heilbon, the wife of the Nashville rabbi of 1859 and 1860.[23]

This "on to America" movement gave impetus to the formation of committees and associations which obtained data on migration and settlement. All were encouraged to unite for travel. Jewish emigrants were particularly enjoined to unite for purposes of observing the dietary laws, the holidays and the ceremonies. Many groups combined so that they might bring with them the Torah Scrolls and ritual objects and that they might have within their midst a cantor or a religious leader.[24] It has been said that the emigrant truly set out with a prayer on his lips. There were editions of prayer books with special prayers for crossing the seas and a ready market necessitated editions in 1842, 1849, 1855, and 1860.[25] Let us not forget that from many villages the Christian and Jew traveled side by side, their differences blotted out in a mutual dream of freedom.

The associations for emigration required a payment for membership which entitled the member to designate one person for emigration. The emigrant could, if necessary, receive a loan from the association which was to be repaid. There were no established synagogal societies to assist the Jewish emigrant as existed in the Christian churches.[26] And there were many who left without permit or passport. The hurried selection and adoption of a surname for one family group consisting of an uncle and eight nephews suggest a probable departure without the necessary legal papers. When informed, as they prepared to sail, that they must acquire a family name, the uncle, known in his native village only as Zadik, chose the name of Levy, the probable name of his father or grandfather. The nephews preferred the name of their native province; so the eight of them became the Nassauers or men from Nassau.[27]

28

As stated earlier, the author has found it necessary to weave into the meager known facts in the lives of our local Jewish settlers the experiences that were common to all emigrants of the 1840's and 1850's. The sentiments and emotions expressed by Abraham Kohn in his diary reveal the sadness of separation from one's family; and, in all likelihood, were the same emotions experienced by the Oppenheimer brothers, the Jessel brothers, the Lande brothers and the Flashman brothers, early Nashville settlers. Kohn wrote on June 15, 1842, "Yesterday morning I began my journey to North America together with my brother Moses . . . It was difficult to leave my dear brothers and sisters and especially my dear Mother. . . Tears are a gift from God. I wept bitterly as I kissed my dear Mother for perhaps the last time."[28]

Mid-nineteenth century travel was at best a risky adventure. It required stamina and fearlessness. The immigrant ships had improved little in over a century; most crossings were in sailing vessels. Only three per cent of the immigrants arriving in New York in 1856 came by steamship. The majority of the ships were freighters which exchanged their cotton, tobacco and timber brought from America for human cargo. Agents chartered the lower decks at a fixed rate per ton of cargo.

There were difficulties to be encountered even before sailing. Waiting for the wind or arrival of freight could delay departure. There were usually more immigrants at the seaports than could be taken care of, so some would be left behind. To those who had walked the hundreds of miles from their homes, this was a great disappointment. Julius Ochs was such a one who had tramped the six hundred miles from his native Frankfort to Bremen in 1845.[29] During the delay at the seaports, the emigrants were besieged by tavern keepers, shipbrokers and land agents as they continued to make their final preparations for the long sea journey of some seven weeks.

Provisions must be taken for the entire trip so it was necessary to have good containers that would withstand the gnawing of rats. At the emigrant provision stores, located near the wharves, could be purchased cooking and eating utensils and hooks and nails that would be used to suspend the cheeses, fish and clothing from the walls of the ship.[30]

Often it was necessary for families to dispose of their few cherished heirlooms. The danger of being robbed was ever present as was the fear that the delayed sailing might be so extended that provisions and money would be exhausted.

Packed like herring into stuffy quarters, the emigrant ship was truly a rat hole where the passengers fought over the use of the stove for cooking and were lucky if they were able to get half-cooked food. Living on moldy bread, spoiled meat and fish, and suffering from a lack of fresh air, it was inevitable that large numbers fell prey to cholera, smallpox and dysentery.[31]

The hygienic conditions were so deplorable and the mortality on emigrant ships so high, that the Senate of the United States appointed a committee to investigate the causes and extent of the situation, to ascertain if legislation was needed for the protection of the passengers. The report of the committee revealed that in the last four months of 1852, of the three hundred twelve vessels with 96,950 passengers arriving in New York port from Europe, 47 of the vessels had cholera, 1933 passengers died at sea, 457 passengers were sent to hospitals and 21,857 had been victims of cholera. Lack of fresh air and partially cooked foods were considered the major causes of mortality. The committee recommended that the cooking be furnished by the ship personnel, and that the sexes be separated to prevent shocking immoralities.[32]

It has been said, and rightly so, that the many dangers facing the American pioneers on their westward march were as nothing when we consider the perils that confronted the nineteenth century emigrant. Undoubtedly, an indomitable faith and hope in the prerogative of all men for a free world drove them on, insensitive to their discomforts but motivated by their dreams. Among such travelers were four European families who resided in Nashville in the decade of the '50's. In the lowly quarters of an emigrant ship in the year 1849, Anna Levy, attended by her husband S., gave birth to their third child Joseph.[33] Michael and Pauline Schwartz, natives of Poland, with daughters

Rebecca, age eleven, Rosy, age nine and Mary, age six, landed in New York about 1850.[34] Three years later another Polish couple Alexander and Jennie Klein with little Simon, three, and Henry, one, arrived in the promised land.[35] And in 1852 from Cracow came David and I. M. Sobel with I. M.'s wife, Yette, and their infant son.[36] For these couples now began the chapter on "life, liberty and the pursuit of happiness."

Excluding the political refugees and the military service evaders, it must be remembered that the immigrant of this period was poor and unworldly. He nursed a burning desire to escape discrimination and to better his economic condition. In many instances his treatment upon arrival would have discouraged the most ardent of freedom seekers. There has never been a time when man was not beset by swindlers and crooks and this plague abounded in the 1850's. They were there at the wharves to fleece the innocent emigrant out of his few remaining possessions. Landlords, railway agents, land sharks descended upon the newcomer, adding to his bewilderment. The emigrant guides suggested so many ways of making any contemplated journey, and the representatives of the competing companies were each so convincing in the expediency and low rates of their own systems. How did one make a choice of river, canal, railroad or coach? A Nashville newspaper wrote, "one of the greatest crimes is the selling of spurious tickets to those bound for points West. Good tickets are sold for passage from New York to Albany but from there on the tickets are worthless . . . in a single day in Albany, one thousand foreigners have been stranded with false tickets."[37]

It was not until 1855 that Castle Garden was created to protect the immigrant from fraudulence. In New York, charitable societies were being established to assist the newcomer. Twenty percent of the Jewish arrivals were dependent on Jewish charities.[38] A society had been established as early as 1843 to induce migration from port cities.[39]

Again it became necessary, in many instances, to remain in New York until money could be saved for a continuance of the journey. Abraham Kohn, from whose diary this writer has pre-

31

viously quoted, wrote so realistically of his efforts to gain a livelihood:

> During this period I was in New York trying in vain to find a job as clerk in a store. But business was too slow and I had to do as all the others; with a bundle on my back, I had to go out into the country, peddling various articles. . . O, misguided fools, led astray by avarice and cupidity! You have left your friends and acquaintances, your relatives and your parents, your home and your fatherland, your language and your customs, your faith and your religion to sell your wares in the wild places of America, in isolated farmhouses and tiny hamlets.[40]

There were many families who were to settle in Nashville during this eventful decade for whom this New York stopover was compulsory. It requires no stretch of the imagination to realize the doubts and apprehensions that grew out of their loneliness. The Russian tailor, Simon Heims, and his wife, Rosa, arriving in New York from a delayed routing through England, where their third child was born, remained residents of this great metropolis for the years 1854 to 1857 or 1858, and during this sojourn were blessed with three more children.[41] We ponder if Mary Lewis was one of those wives to whose care her[42] three children, born in New York between 1849 and 1853, were entrusted while husband Solomon trudged the New York villages selling his wares, but taking the time in 1852 at Troy, New York, to apply for his citizenship.[43] The Robert Blums, the Jacob Ellis', the Henry Cohens, the Michael Schwartz', and the S. Levys[44] were some of the immigrant families who settled in New York for the first few years of their American residence.

There were other ports of entry which offered the newcomers temporary shelter. Young Sigmund Godhelp, age 17, arrived in Baltimore in 1853 from his native Hesse and two years later his younger brother, Jacob, by then also 17, arrived.[45] I. Flatau arrived at the port of Boston in 1854.[46] New Orleans was the port of entry for Harris Abrahams, the Polish youth who had stowed away on a sailing vessel out of Liverpool.[47] Charleston was the likely seaport that welcomed A. Livingston and wife from Poland for it was in South Carolina that the two Livingston children, Marcus and Louis, were born.[48] To Nashville from Georgia came the Henry Spitz family. Mrs. Spitz, nee Caroline Phillips, landed in Charleston with her first husband, G. L. Levy, in 1849 to join her husband's brothers who were the first Jewish settlers in Augusta, Georgia, in 1840.[49] The Levy brothers achieved much prominence in their community. One brother, Isaac, served as chief sheriff, and another brother, Samuel, was Judge of the Superior Court and also Judge of the Court of the Ordinary.[50]

It was a time of shifting populations; the country was on the move. New lands gained from the Mexican war, bolstered by the discovery of gold in California, triggered the westward expansion. Tennesseans pioneered in Texas; and from the North, the East and Europe, came new settlers to Tennessee. By river, by canal, by stage and by the very latest in land travel, the railroad, the population moved. In the two decades of 1840 and 1850, the traffic was largely waterborne. The 125 steamboats on the Mississippi and Ohio rivers in 1825 had grown to one thousand by 1860.[51] Nashville had a weekly service to New Orleans; ship arrivals and departures were reported daily in the newspapers.[52] The success of the Erie Canal had led to canal building throughout the country culminating into a nation of interlocking waterways. The cheap one cent a mile travel rate by river and canal more than compensated for the snail's pace of three miles an hour.[53] There was an ever present danger of explosion due in large measure to the snags and bars in the rivers. In 1858, forty-seven steamboats were sunk on western rivers, nineteen were burned up and nine exploded.[54] And in 1860 H. Cronstine gave an eye witness account of his experiences in the collision of two steamers on the Ohio river.[55] An unknown immigrant has left us a graphic description of travel between New Orleans and Cincinnati. "I went by boat to Louisville and Cincinnati, a distance of 1600 miles on the Mississippi and Ohio Rivers . . . the Mississippi was very muddy—the Ohio much clearer and had more houses and towns . . . it cost $7.00 for second class cabin passage . . . we stopped twice a day to take in wood that was burned—25 cords in 24 hours . . . the passengers are mostly German and Irish immigrants."[56] The German Jew, I. J. Benjamin, made a cross country tour of America in the years 1859-1862 and wrote of his experiences in the large established Jewish communities. He gave the distance between New Orleans and Cincinnati as 800 miles.[57]

The largely German cities of Cincinnati and St. Louis attracted the newcomers. On one day in 1852, one thousand German and Irish immigrants arrived in Cincinnati from New Orleans.[58] By 1860 the German element constituted 30% of Cincinnati. An early traveler had written that there were so many sign boards in German that "one felt he was in Hamburg."[59] The first and oldest Jewish congregation west of the Alleghenies was here and it served as a focal point for Jews who came from distances as far as New Orleans for the High Holy Days. Drawn to a place that resembled in many ways their native Bavaria, were the three Sulzbacher brothers, Henry, Marx and Martin. As early as 1840 Martin was listed as one of the incorporators of the second established synagogue in Cincinnati, Congregation B'nai Yeshurun.[60] Here he remained until 1849 when the family moved to Pulaski, Tennessee, for a brief residence before coming to Nashville in the early 1850's. Mrs. Sulzbacher was Dorothy Hollstein, daughter of an early German Jewish immigrant who had arrived in Cincinnati in the late 1820's.[61] Another prominent Jewish Dutch family in early Cincinnati was the Le Jeune family who had emigrated from Amsterdam to New York about 1820. Here Bernard Le Jeune had married Esther Myers, a granddaughter of the same Benjamin Myers whose daughter was the first recorded Jewish child born in Nashville in 1795. In 1830 Bernard was a signer of the charter for the oldest synagogue west of the Alleghenies, congregation Bene Israel[62] of Cincinnati. A few years after Bernard's death, his widow married Jacob Hyman. It was not until the late 1850's that the Hymans settled in Nashville where their two daughters Rebecca (Mrs. Sam Powers) and Henrietta (Mrs. Michael Powers) were already living and where in 1861 a third daughter Isabella was to be married to Myer Joseph at the outbreak of the Civil War.[63]

English Jewry had been largely responsible for the creation of the Jewish community in Cincinnati. As a consequence it continued to draw many immigrants, Englishmen of Plymouth, Portsmouth and London. Prominent among these were the three Powers brothers of Portsmouth and London, both places being recorded as places of birth. As mere boys they had left their native England to ship out as cabin boys on sailing vessels. The sea, too, had its charm for their father Moses. At the mother's death, he invested in a cargo of silk and embarked with it for America. Off the coast of Bermuda the vessel was wrecked and the precious cargo lost. Happily, father Powers survived and made his way to Louisville, Kentucky.[64] A Nashville legend relates that about 1840, three English sailors arrived in Nashville. Two of these were Michael and Louis Powers and the third a good Irish friend named Burns.[65]

At the beginning of the 1860's the Isaac Frank family arrived in Nashville by way of Cincinnati.[66] Via Pennsylvania came the Sam Brodies, the Louis Morgansterns and the Robert Blums, the latter family also living briefly in Ohio.[67] Henry Harris not only had lived in Pennsylvania but had applied for citizenship in Missouri in 1844[68] before beginning a permanent Nashville residence. The M. Rice family's arrival about 1845 followed a short sojourn in Michigan.[69] Probably the most traveled couples of this decade were the Samuel Levicks and the H. Livingstons. The two Levick children, Rachael and Eva, were born in 1854 and 1855 respectively in California also the birthplace of young Louis Livingston. Sister Jane Livingston was born in Arkansas.[70] How unfortunate that the stories of their probable overland route adventure were never recorded. Near the close of the Civil War another 49'er joined the Nashville Jewish community. He was Morris Fishel, a native of Bavaria, who also had lived for many years in the Queen City of the Ohio, Cincinnati.

The oldest and in many instances the only direct mode of travel between Nashville and surrounding towns was the coach line. As early as 1802 the traveller Michaux found the road from Knoxville to Nashville over the Cumberland Mountains "as wide and as well beaten as those in the environs of Philadelphia."[71]

The four hundred eighty mile Natchez Trace road from New Orleans was considerably less than the route via the Mississippi, Ohio and Cumberland rivers,[72] but the cheaper rates gave water travel an advantage. In 1850 the one hundred eighty mile coach trip from Louisville to Nashville required thirty-three hours and cost twelve dollars.[73] By 1845 there were four hundred ten miles of macademized roads in middle Tennessee.[74] The hard surfaced roads increased the speed of coaches from three or four miles an hour to seven and eight miles. It is doubtful if the stage offered more in comfort than did the river boats. The roads were dusty and the coaches often overcrowded. A Cincinnati resident in July 1854 proposed the following to travelers, "One should have brandy or a small piece of opium or gum camphor to be useful in stage sickness."[75]

Inevitably and unwillingly, Nashville welcomed the railroad. At the beginning of the decade there were only nine thousand miles of railway in the entire country; Tennessee boasted one hundred twelve miles with an additional seven hundred forty-eight under construction.[76] Legislation had been enacted in 1846 for a railroad in Nashville; but it was Christmas Day 1850 before the first engine arrived by boat from Cincinnati.[77] The age of speed had arrived; railroad time averaged twenty-five to thirty miles an hour. At the sometimes increased rate of thirty and thirty-five miles the passengers were treated to much jolting and noise. Delays in schedules and poor connections often necessitated the use of train, coach and river for a single destination. Passenger cars were uncomfortable, and in many areas the newly arrived immigrants took advantage of the lowest possible rates for a box car service of rude seats and no windows. In winter there were extra value opportunities in the use of passenger power when the engines failed to start. Both river and rail travel had their relaxing moments when one could fish or just enjoy himself while the firemen stopped and cut the necessary wood.[78]

The new fangled travel caught on. Ten thousand rode the Ohio and Pennsylvania Railway in the first week of April 1854.[79] The daily schedule of trains appeared in the local papers. By leaving at eleven thirty each evening one could arrive in Chattanooga the following morning at nine fifty. There were equally adequate facilities for transportation to connecting lines that served Atlanta, New Orleans and Memphis. By 1860 Nashville boasted four railroads,[80] and Tennessee had a system of 1,253 miles of railway.[81] The railroad was here to stay even though it spelled ultimate doom to the river and coach travel.

Undoubtedly, the young unattached immigrant found his way to this capital city by trudging the wearisome turnpikes and country roads. J. Swartzenberg, Bernard Klein, Isidor Fisher and J. Isaacs peddled their wares as they pushed ever deeper and further south.[82]

This was travel in the 1850's. We need no bold or daring imagination to conclude that in such a manner and under such circumstances our European Jewish immigrants arrived in Nashville.

CHAPTER III

A Time to Build Up

"Hear O Israel, the Lord our God, the Lord is One."

THIS IS the *Shema*, the primary theme of the Jewish faith. A changeless and enduring belief in the Oneness of God is the core of Judaism regardless of the practices of its followers. Judaism is also a way of life, and the Jew has only to turn to Torah[1] and Talmud[2] for a guide to every day living. Here may be found the rules of conduct for all from birth to death, in not only one's relationship with God, but in one's personal life and one's treatment of his fellow man. Judaism is the oldest of the monotheistic religions. In its four thousand year history it has seen and undergone changes. Following the dispersion in the year 70 C.E., it substituted for the sacrificial cult of the Temple a worship of personal prayers based on the ethical concepts of the Prophets.

It was not until the ghetto walls opened and the Jew began to participate in the secular world that the century old traditions and customs were questioned, and changes and reforms introduced. This reform movement had its birthplace in Germany in the early nineteenth century. In America the first reform congregation was established in Charleston, South Carolina, in the 1820's but was short lived. The 1840's and 1850's witnessed the growth of several reform congregations as the movement received impetus through the activities of two great reformers, Rabbi Isaac M. Wise and Rabbi David Einhorn. These innovations did not appear on the local scene until the middle of the 1860's as large numbers of Jews moved into the area. The story of reform versus orthodoxy is a chronicle of another era and for the antebellum Jew we need concern ourselves only with the traditional Jew who wrote into the charter of the first Nashville synagogue, "the mode of worship be according to the form used

38

and adopted by the Polish Israelites."

The seventh and eighth censuses revealed no Jewish congregations in Tennessee, but there were three in the state by 1860 when the eighth census erroneously reported none. Whether by coincidence or planning, the act which created a synagogue for Nashville also authorized one for Memphis.[3]

Prior to 1850 the Jews met for services in the home of Isaac Garritson on South Summer Street.[4] Undoubtedly, there were the daily morning and evening prayers and Sabbath service. It was unthinkable that a Jew would neglect the important High Holy Days of the New Year (*Rosh Ha Shonah*) or the awesome Day of Atonement (*Yom Kippur*). The *Kaddish* recited on the anniversary of the death of a loved one had a very deep meaning for the Jew and undoubtedly brought to the home service many stragglers who may have been remiss in daily worship attendance. Mr. Henry Harris, son-in-law of Isaac Garritson, served as the reader for the group.

The first recorded evidence of any organized Jewish group was written in the Davidson County Deeds to Property.[5] In July 1851, Isaac Garritson, Jacob Mitchell and Michael Powers, trustees of the Hebrew Benevolent Burial Association known as Shield of David, purchased for a cemetery three 3/160 acres of land on the Buena Vista Pike, one and one-half miles from the city. The price of $377.36 was to be paid in a cash payment of $125.78 and the balance in three payments over a two year period. In the history of American Jewry it will be noted that benevolent societies usually predated the establishment of a synagogue. One year later, in August 1852, Mr. Garritson wrote to the prominent Rabbi of Philadelphia, Isaac Leeser, "It is very gratifying for me to be able to inform you that we have established here last year a Hebrew Benevolent Society . . . our Society is at present very small, yet numbering only five families and about eight young men. . . ."

It follows naturally that we ask, "Who were these five families and eight young men?" As no roster of the membership of this society has been found, the author can only list the names of those persons who were living in Nashville between the years

1850 and 1852 and whose names appeared on either the first deed to the cemetery property issued in 1851 or the second deed which transferred the property from the Benevolent Society to the Congregation Mogen David in 1853.[6]

The families were those of Isaac Garritson and his son-in-law, Henry Harris, which may be considered as one, Jacob Mitchell about whom this writer can only conjecture, M. Sulzbacher, E. Wolf, M. Rice and Louis Hanf. The names of only six young men appeared on these two deeds, and they were Michael Powers, A. Lande, Louis Sohn, E. Franklin, H. Jessel and M. Elsbach. The author, after careful consideration, would suggest as the likely two remaining young men, Louis Powers a brother of Michael, and David Elsbach a brother of Max. And yet, any one of the following might have been one of the eight young men, M. Cohn, S. Marks, M. Oppenheimer, A. B. Oppenheimer or Sinai Nathan. The last two names appeared in both the charter to the congregation issued in 1854 and in the 1850 census records for Nashville.

The arrival date for Nashville's first Rabbi, Alexander Iser, a native of Poland who had been living in New York, is indefinite. He probably came for the High Holy Days in the fall of 1852 but the earliest recorded information appeared in a Jewish national monthly, *The Occident*, in June 1853. Iser was described as an excellent scholar, highly recommended, and his discourse on the Passover rated "very interesting."[7] For his varied and busy congregational services Iser was paid $600 per annum.

The benevolent group had been transformed into a congregation of thirty members by the fall of 1853 when it petitioned the State for a charter of incorporation. The third reading of the petition passed the State Senate on December 5, 1853, but the omissions of the five names, E. Wolf, A. Lande, L. Sohn, S. Nathan and H. Jessel amended the first petition[8]; so that it was held over for the legislature of the following year which legally granted a charter on March 2, 1854.

The congregation continued to meet in a room offered gratuitously by Isaac Garritson. They were also indebted to him for the suggestion, Mogen David, for the name of the congregation in honor so it was said of Davidson County.[9]

The author would like to mention the many discrepancies that were noted in the recording of names. The early Nashville historian, W. W. Clayton, referred to this early Jewish benefactor as Isaac Gershon. Undoubtedly Clayton's information was received orally from a German whose heavy guttural utterance of the name Garritson fell upon his ears as Gershon. In no other record could the name Gershon be found. The name Garritson appeared with many variations in spelling and in a few instances was listed as Garrison. A petitioner of the first congregational charter in 1854, who was also a member of the Board of Trustees listed on the exchange of cemetery property in 1853, was Louis Sohn. He may or may not have been the Louis Cohn who announced his intention of becoming a citizen in the January term 1855 of the Davidson County Circuit Court.[10] Very definitely, the listing of the name A. E. Frankland on the synagogue charter was an error. A. E. Frankland, discussed in chapter one, had resided in Nashville in the 1840's but in 1854 was an active member of the Memphis, Tennessee, congregation serving as its secretary. The Nashville man was Elias Franklin whose name was recorded correctly on the deed to the cemetery property. The letters I and J had an annoying way of being substituted for each other and E. Wolf was undecided about the inclusion of an e on the end of his name so that he appeared in court records, newspapers and deeds to property as both Wolf and Wolfe. The mysteries contained in these century old records truly require, in a historian, greatly developed occult powers.

Another interesting evidence of misspelling, undoubtedly due to foreign enunciation, was found in the first charter issued to Kaal A. Kodesh Mogen David in 1854. This was corrected in a new charter issued October 31, 1855 naming the congregation correctly as Kahl Kodesh Mogen David.[11]

By 1857 the growing congregation had rented a room on North Market Street for five years and reported to the national Jewish periodicals that,[12] "it had been fitted up in handsome style." The *hazzan* (reader), Alexander Iser, had decided to go

41

into business for himself, a practice which appeared quite common amongst the fleeting and shifting *hazzanim* (readers) of that decade. There was a scarcity of trained men available for positions as religious leaders. Synagogues were mushrooming everywhere, and the supply did not equal the demand. The Jewish traveler, I. J. Benjamin, quickly discerned this lamentable condition and wrote, "Jewish congregations turn a shoemaker, a tailor, a furrier or a butcher into a shepherd of souls who can conduct services, supervise observance of the law concerning food, can preach and can write without the least knowledge of Judaism or its sacred writings."[13] This dearth of rabbis and religious teachers led Rabbi Isaac M. Wise to also write, "Reverend Doctors grow out of rocks and prairies in this country . . . it soon will be a shame for a honest man to be styled Reverend Doctor."[14]

When Alexander Iser decided to forsake his scholarly calling for the prosaic but apparently more remunerative field of business, the Nashville congregation followed the common practice and inserted the following notice in the *Asmonean:*

> Congregation K. K. Mogen David desirous of engaging a suitable person to act as schochet, Hazzan, Mohel and teach Hebrew—salary $300 to $400 per annum besides an increase from members. Candidate applying will do so in person at own expense showing testimonials as to qualifications and moral character. D. Elsbach, secretary.[15]

In the fall of 1857 the services of the Reverend Emanuel Marenson were engaged.[16] He had been a candidate and quite likely the only one answering the weekly advertisement. His acceptable manner of preaching sermons and reading the prayers merited his election for a year.

The following account in a local paper was indicative of the lack of knowledge of the Jewish High Holy Days among the Christian editors. "Yesterday and today constituted the New Year Holidays in the Jewish calendar. The usual church ceremonies were observed yesterday in the synagogue on Market Street and will be continued today. Next Monday week is the

Day of Atonement and will be observed by this people with the usual Festivals."[17]

At the annual meeting the following year, 1858, the congregation reported, "Mr. E. Marcusson who was with us last year . . . has been reelected for the ensuing year."[18] Again the reader may be confused over the identities of the Reverends Marenson and Marcusson. From the statement that Marcusson was reelected for another year and from the possession of the first name initialed E. by both, it may be concluded that another error in either spelling or printing has bequeathed to later historians and readers another of its perplexing riddles.

Under Marcusson's guidance the congregation grew in membership and completed the building of a *mikveh* (ritual bath). Marcusson was quite proficient in his many congregational duties; his ability as *Mohel* (one who circumcises) was so described, "This ceremony has been performed by him in the presence of old and experienced persons who say they never saw a better one."[19]

Circumcision dates back to the days of Abraham. In Genesis we read, "This is My covenant which ye shall keep between Me and you and thy seed after thee; every male among you shall be circumcised."[20] This covenant at Sinai was binding upon the Jew. There were instances when a *Mohel* who must be specially trained for this ceremony, would be imported from many miles at great expense to fulfill the obligation of the covenant. Moses Lieberman, an active member of Congregation Adath Israel of Louisville, Kentucky, and an uncle of Simon Lieberman who settled in Nashville about 1859, was for many years the ony *Mohel* in the state of Kentucky.[21] And there were not so few boys born in the years 1857-1859 in Nashville who very conceivably were recipients of Marcusson's skillful services. These probably included Jacob and Marx Levy, Samuel and Willie Ellis, Nathan and Charles Shyer, Jacob Schwartz, Henry Powers, Solomon Lande, Myer Cohen, Abraham Bloomstein, Solomon Harris, Samuel Lewis and L. Adler.[22] The girl child was named in the synagogue at the first service of the reading of the Torah following birth. Marcusson found the time to also serve as the local agent for the national Jewish weekly, *The Jewish Messenger*.

In the spring of 1859 the notices for a replacement were again printed in the papers, as Marcusson had departed. A native of Prussia who had been living in Poughkeepsie, New York, was the successful candidate. He was a Rabbi Heilbon whose given name appeared in different listings as Jonas and as Isaac. Under his leadership the congregation flourished; services were well attended. Standing room only was the report at the High Holy Day services. The beautification of the Ark was a project completed at this time. The capable R. D. Blum, described as "a superior and masterly engraver," presented to the congregation two large plates upon which were engraved in large gilt letters the Ten Commandments. These plates were arranged over the Ark (where hand written Torahs are kept) and beneath the large plates was a small one bearing Blum's name and the date of the gift.[23]

Jonas Heilbon inaugurated in Nashville the first religious school patterned after the Sunday School.[24] It was not only traditional but it was a requirement that every Jewish boy be taught Hebrew. When many of the world were illiterate, the Jewish child could read. This learning began in the fifth year and continued at least until the thirteenth year when every boy observed his *Bar Mitsvah*. This ceremony marked a boy's acceptance of his responsibility for his religious duties and for his own actions.

In July 1860 after an illness of ten years, Phoebe Heilbon, a native of Cornville, England, and the Rabbi's wife, passed away. The congregation by acceding to his request to return to his former home in New York was once again seeking a rabbi. The affairs of the congregation for the next decade were written for posterity in the recurring advertisements for a "Hazzan Schochet and Mohel for the K. K. Mogen David in Nashville."

Fortunately one letter from a candidate, dated March 12, 1862, has been preserved. Alb. Rosenfeld, a native of Hungary then holding a post in Peoria, Illinois, announced by letter that he was a candidate for the vacant office advertised by the K. K. Mogen David. He was desirous of knowing the kind of customs employed in the synagogue, whether German, Polish or American. Further questions concerned the number of children, the hours of instruction and the amount of the salary. Mr. Rosenfeld then listed his qualifications and agreed to sending documents that would testify to his ability. The added postscript revealing the candidate's quest for a salubrious climate said, "You will please to inform me . . . whether your city and vicinity are in a healthy location."[25]

Prior to Heilbon's departure, a cleavage in the Jewish group culminated in the establishment of a second congregation. This was a common occurrence in the history of American synagogues. Differing languages, customs and liturgy inevitably created discord; each member crusaded for the establishment of his own familiar ritual, born out of his own experiences. The writer, I. J. Benjamin, placed much of the blame for dissension on the unlimited freedom which religious congregations enjoyed in America. "The slightest insult or an unsuccessful bid for congregational office would lead disappointed men into founding new congregations."[26] The conditions that precipitated the schism in the Nashville congregation are unknown today. In November 1859 a petition was read in the Tennessee Legislature to permit the Jews of Nashville to purchase burial grounds and erect a synagogue under the name of Ohava Emes (Lovers of Truth). The petitioners were L. Powers, Samuel Cohen, A. Klein, Samuel Powers, H. Spritz (should be Spitz), S. Levick, A. Iser (first *Hazzan*) and H. H. Goldberg. The charter was granted March 12, 1860.[27] It was a house divided, Mogen David versus Ohava Emes.

The synagogue, since its inception, has been more than a house of worship; it has served as a meeting place for study, discussion and leisure time activities. Much of the Sabbath day was devoted to a reading and explanation of the Torah and the Talmud; it was a day of release from the problems of the workaday world. Suddenly this new American, this transplanted Jew, faced an economic problem when he dared observe a Sabbath on a day different from his Christian neighbor. Furthermore, his non-observance of the first day of the week as a day of rest frequently brought him into conflict with the law. To the Jew his Sabbath was a day of rest, of peace, of joy, quite in contrast to the restrictive Sunday described by Randal McGavock, a prominent Nashvillian of the 1850's as, "Sunday is always a long and dull day."[28]

In Jewish life the home was ever a little sanctuary. On the doorposts were placed the *Mazuzas*, small metal or wood scrolls which contained the *Shema*. This reminded one as he left or entered his home of the unity of God. Since the home was established through marriage, it followed that the ceremony and rites of marriage were sacred and holy. Divorce was frowned upon, and Rabbi Leeser commented at great length on the first Jewish divorce obtained in Cleveland in the early 1850's.[29] The following couples were among those who were joined in wedlock in that eventful decade: Louis Bloomstein to Rebecca Greenbaum, David Elsbach to Sarah Lipman, Sinai Nathan to Sophia Stein, Julius Ochs to Bertha Levy, Nathan Cline to Emma Laufer, Samuel Lyons to Elizabeth Isaaks, Jacob Lyons to S A. Delisser, Samuel Abrahams to Teresa Sayers, Samuel Cohen to Caroline Schiff, David Aaron to Mary Louis, Myer Joseph to Isabella Hyman.[30]

Neither the Jewish rabbi nor the *hazzan* were empowered to perform marriages in Tennessee until March 1879 when the Tennessee legislature authorized Jewish rabbis to solemnize the rites of marriage.[31] The services of a justice of the peace were required at all the Jewish weddings in the 1850's to legalize the religious ceremony performed by the rabbi or *hazzan*.

Judaism teaches that it is a *mitsvah* (commandment) to give aid when needed. The word *tzedaka* which refers to charity, actually means righteousness. When the first group of twenty-three Jews landed in Niew Amsterdam (New York) in 1654 and were repulsed by the Dutch Governor Peter Stuyvesant, permission to remain was granted only after a solemn promise that the Jew would never be a burden on the community. During the early settlement of this country it was customary for a church or religious organization to take care of its own poor, so Stuyvesant's requirement was a normal one. Until the recent affiliation of Jewish welfare agencies with the larger overall community fund-raising agencies, the Jew had taken care of his own charity. The success of this completely Jewish undertaking was reflected in an editorial in a local paper as early as 1854 which commented, "The Jew is seldom found in hospitals and never in poor houses."[32] When a request came for help, be it for the establishment of schools or a bride's dowry, or to fight discrimination or to aid the sufferers of pogroms, the Jew reached into his pockets and gave.

Undoubtedly, there were many instances that taxed the meager resources of the local community. Most often it was a loan to a friend that enabled him to go into a business of peddling, but it might be free burials for the impoverished, Hebrew lessons for a needy child, or aid to the widowed and fatherless. When Joseph Stein died in 1858 leaving a young wife and year old child, Isaac Garritson, David Elsbach and Henry Harris appealed to the court for a settlement of the estate that would allow the wife and child an adequate sustenance.[33]

With the arrival of more and more needy immigrants, it became apparent that a society dedicated purely to benevolence was necessary. The organization of this group, known as the Young Men's Hebrew Benevolent Society, occurred in August 1859. However, the charter was not issued until March 5, 1860.[34] By then an enthusiastic and active membership had sponsored a charity ball as a fund-raising affair.[35] The membership drew its strength from the younger element. Its incorporators were Benjamin Lyons, S. Margolins, David Aaron, P. Flashman, S. Lieberman, L. Solomon and J. Emanuel.

The services of the women were requested on many occasions, and in the early '60's they organized their own society for "the purpose of relieving the needy and distressed, attending upon the sick and for such worthy and charitable purposes as the constitution may provide." The charter for the Ladies' Hebrew Benevolent Society was not issued until February 1870, and those listed in the charter were Dorah Sulzbacher, Bertha Lusky, Bertha Schwarz, Ida Bernheim, Sarah Felderman (Feldman), C. Karger, M. Cronstein and Sophia Shyer.[36]

There was no national organization that unified or served as spokesman for the Jew. The B'nai Brith, a benevolent and philanthropic order, had its origin in New York City in 1843 but did not appear on the local scene until 1863.[37] The group was chartered by the State on October 24, 1865, as Maimonides Lodge number forty-six and the incorporators were D. Aaron, J. Loeb, A. Lande, S. Weil, A. Landsberg, E. Wolf and J. Mann.[38]

A second benevolent society, an affiliate of another national group, was organized in Nashville at the close of the Civil War. Its main object was to support widows and orphans. It received its charter on February 19, 1868, as King Solomons Lodge number six of the Independent Order of Brith Abraham.[39]

The Jewish communities avidly read and enthusiastically discussed the Jewish papers; they also eagerly sought the advice of its editors, the majority of whom were able and consecrated rabbis. Isaac Leeser, an unauthorized chief Rabbi of American Jewry, was the man from whom Isaac Garritson sought Jewish books. Leeser served as *hazzan* of the prominent Philadelphia congregation, Mikveh Israel, for thirty-nine years and he edited a monthly paper, *The Occident,* which first appeared in 1843. Robert Lyons, a layman, edited the *Asmonean* for the years 1849 until his premature death in 1858. Rabbi Isaac M. Wise established and edited two papers, *The Israelite* in 1854 and *Die Deborah* a German paper in 1855. *The Jewish Messenger* appeared in 1857 and was edited by the New York Rabbi, Samuel Isaacs. The great Baltimore reformer and Rabbi, David Einhorn, began publication of a German paper, *The Sinai,* in 1856. It was unlikely that the *San Francisco* Gleaner, initiated in 1858 by Rabbi Juluis Eckman, attracted any local readers at such great distance.

These Rabbis used their papers as lecture platforms. They instructed and informed their readers of the international, national and local events, political, religious and social. They had encyclopedic information on questions of ritual and liturgy and were perhaps the arbitrators in many local squabbles. Rabbi Wise pleaded with his readers to never evade or deny the issue of being a Jew. "Christians respect those who respect themselves and practice their faith."[40]

Many requests for relief and cooperation came via the printed page. In an editorial in *The Israelite* on August 7, 1857, Rabbi Wise urged "Agitate"—"Call Meetings, engage the press in your favor." The turmoil was precipitated by an American treaty with the Swiss Government which discriminated against the Jew. As a result of Wise's appeal, the Nashville Jewry called a mass meeting at the synagogue on Sunday October 18, 1857, and resolutions adopted read, "That as citizens and Israelites we protest the articles adopted in the treaty whereby citizens of Switzerland are deprived of certain rights while living in that country and that the President take steps to secure the same privilege for the Jew as are enjoyed by all citizens." A committee was appointed to confer with United States Senators to plead this cause in the Senate.[41]

The first national organization to speak for American Jewry, The Board of Delegates of the American Israelites, was founded in 1859 as a protest against the abduction in 1858 of the six year old Italian child, Edgar Mortara. Years earlier the child had been quite ill and a devout Catholic nurse had secretly baptized him. The act was never divulged until the nurse was dismissed from her position. When the Catholic authorities were informed, they spirited the child away. Not only world Jewry but the Protestant world was aroused and incensed at this indignity. The child was never returned to his parents.

In the fomenting '50's, America seethed with the fiery zeal of saving men's souls. These were active years for church workers; it was a time of revivals and camp meetings. The Society for Ameliorating the Condition of the Jews had been organized in the 1820's for the sole purpose of converting the Jew, but its missionaries and periodicals had failed to attract many. Leeser lashed out at the Society terming it a fraud and advising the Jews to shun it.[42] And Wise censured the activities of a converted Jew, S. Bonhomme who had been energetic in his efforts to convert Jews in Louisville and Nashville.[43] At an anniversary celebration in New York City in 1854, the Society reported eight regular missionaries and eight part-time, all converted Hebrews, and announced that twenty-nine converts had been made during the year. The Society found no Jews needing relief.[44] This condition certainly did not contribute to the success of the Society. The efforts of this group seemed to spark in the Jew a stubborn and persistent loyalty to his faith.

In addition to the problem of fighting conversion, Nashville Jewry experienced a perplexing situation in the treatment of Christian converts to Judaism. Converts have always been accepted, but Judaism has considered it improper to urge one of another faith to become a Jew. Adah Menken, celebrated and beautiful actress of this era, was a devout and loyal convert to Judaism. She resented the humiliations and discriminations heaped upon her people, and she observed in her life-time much of the discipline of her new faith. Neither glory nor profit could tempt her to perform on the stage on the holy day of *Yom Kippur* which she spent in prayer and fasting.[45]

In March 1856 Rabbi Bernard Illowy, a staunch champion of Orthodoxy and a great Talmudist, was invited to Nashville to render an opinion on the authenticity of a woman's conversion to Judaism. This moving and profound story, written so eloquently by this understanding mediator, would lose much of its soul stirring beauty in the retelling; so permit yourself to step back in time to that eventful day, March 23, 1856, when the congregation Mogen David resolved unanimously to abide by the following decision:

> This day came before me a question concerning a deceased person whose right to burial some have contested and I decided according to the knowledge with which the Lord has favored me. But that all men might know the justice of the case, I will explain all which belongs to the inquiry and the answer which I have given thereto.
>
> A certain Jew, a native of Holland, whom it is not necessary to mention by name, took unto himself a Gentile wife, and left his own country with her to seek a home in another portion of the world, to wit, some part of America; and it came to pass as he had lived with her in a manner contrary to our law for some years his spirits disturbed him for the wrong he had done; and he moved the heart of his wife to forsake the false belief of a

strange god and she said, 'Moses is true—his law is true. I will join the Lord and your people shall be my people and your God, my God.' So in the year 5599 (1838) they returned to Holland to the city of Amsterdam but no Rabbi would convert the wife because a royal ordinance ruled that no one could quit his native religion, but they told them to go to a small city where it might be done quietly and no one would know. And so they went to the town of Maarsche and she was converted, doing all the requirements appertaining to female—they were then legally married according to the law of Moses and Israel. But the Judge would not give them a certificate as he feared having transgressed the royal mandate. And then the man and his wife returned to America and it is now fifteen years since they settled in Nashville where they have done what is right and good in the eyes of the Lord. She was pious, modest, strict, nothing prohibited ever entered her house, she kept the Sabbath, she opened her hand to the poor and showed kindness to the living and the dead. She educated her husband's wife's daughter in the fear of God and taught her well what the daughters of Israel have to observe and the daughter emulated the deeds of the mother.

In the past week she became ill and called her husband to her bedside and together after him repeated the Shema six times and then her spirit fled.

When her husband desired to bury her, some objected as they wanted proof of her conversion. The rabbinical authority says that no proof need be presented for a person whose life and deeds showed she was a proselyte. She lived and died a real Israelite. Those who showed kindness to bury her did well, and those who objected were wrong. May her soul be bound up with the souls of all pious men and women.[46]

This modern Ruth who forsake the faith of her fathers for the one God of her husband was Mrs. Isaac Garritson, the wife of Nashville's prominent and devout pre-civil war Jew.

The Baptist, Christian, Episcopal, Lutheran, Methodist, Presbyterian, Catholic and Jewish religions[47] were divided on issues of creed, ritual and liturgy but they were united in matters involving aid to the less fortunate and downtrodden. Within all religious groups, benevolent organizations, aiding the poor,

the widowed and the orphaned, blossomed during the 1840's and
1850's. Governments took cognizance of the blind, the deaf, the
mentally ill. Reforms were introduced in the treatment of criminals. Religion could not be divorced from the economic and
social scene. A time to build up could be accomplished only by
following the prophetic injunction, "seek justice, love mercy and
walk humbly with God."

CHAPTER IV

A Time to Plant

A GRICUTURE was the dominant industry in Tennessee in the 1850's[1] and Nashville was situated in the heart of its most productive area. However, it was not among the predominant farming class that the Jew was to be found; this occupation for many centuries had been *verboten*. It was trade which attracted the immigrant just as it had lured a Frenchman in 1710, and in 1786, Lardner Clark with his ten pack team of "needles, pins, calico and unbleached linens." Tennessee, one of the wealthiest states in the country in 1860, possessed property which was surpassed in value by only five states, Illinois, New York, Ohio, Pennsylvania and Virginia.[2] And Davidson, the richest county in the state, its property valued at $84,898,053, surpassed Shelby County by $3,000,000.[3]

Nashville, favorably situated on a high bluff commanding a view of a navigable river, had early in its history been recognized as a trade center for the surrounding agricultural country.[4] A local paper in 1845 acclaimed Nashville as the wholesale center in dry goods and groceries for Tennessee, Alabama and Kentucky.[5] This early preeminence was bolstered during the 50's by both the establishment of railway facilities and the internal improvement of roads, river beds and bridges. By 1860 Nashville had achieved an enviable position as the most important dry goods market south of Philadelphia.[6] From three wholesale houses doing an annual business of $125,000 in 1850, the dry goods jobbing trade of twelve establishments in 1860 had grown into an annual trade of $2,225,000.[7]

There were no Jewish owners of exclusively wholesale companies either in dry goods, hardware, drugs, shoes or clothing. Undoubtedly, the capital investment required for such enterprises made this venture prohibitive. There were, however, many Jews listed in the five business directories, 1853-1860, whose undertakings were of a combined wholesale and retail status. An analysis of these businesses, which were overwhelmingly devoted to the clothing trade, leads to the conclusion that the proprietors were operating retail stores at wholesale prices.

Much has been written of the beginnings of the Jew in the American business world via the peddler's pack. Undoubtedly, many of Nashville's early Jewish merchants learned the ways of America, trudging by foot the muddy and impassable roads. Later through the diligent and slow accumulation of savings which secured for them the purchase of a horse and buggy, they were able to bring to the isolated rural area not only a breath of the city but a more complete stock of merchandise. They were well received, housed and fed. In exchange for their trinkets, calico and patent medicines they often received eggs, fodder and chickens which could be turned into a neat profit for the purchase of more merchandise. The Jewish traveler, I. J. Benjamin, made this observation of peddling, "This business is not at all in disrepute in America; the Yankee was always engaged in it and the farmer who then had no opportunity to find goods at his door, received the peddler with hospitality."[8]

The census reports of 1850 and 1860 plus the business directories of the decade revealed the names of twenty-six local Jews for whom peddling provided a livelihood.[9] Unquestionably, there were others living in Nashville who escaped tabulation by the census takers because of the traveling demands of a rural selling circuit. And too, it must be noted that the fee for the inclusion of a name in any Nashville business directory would exclude many residents in addition to peddlers. The census returns for 1860 reported 167 peddlers in all of Tennessee[10] and beyond doubt or question Jewry cannot lay claim to all of them.

Many of the peddlers of the hinterlands supplied the small town merchants when their stocks were low. There were some, however, who never left the city; they vended their wares from door to door or collected bottles, rags and junk for sale to large users of such merchandise. A local advertiser wishing to purchase rags appealed to such gatherers with "it is no disgrace to save."[11]

From peddler to second-hand clothing dealer was the next step up the business ladder. This was not only a trade in which the Jew had engaged in Europe but it was a business which was experiencing a flourishing and prosperous era in this country due in part to the great immigration. It required a small investment to repair and clean old clothes that could be resold to many who must economize. One name is listed in this ante bellum era as a dealer in second hand clothing. L. Lindoman, 83 North College Street, was listed in the 1853 business directory.

The clothing business attracted the largest number of Nashville's Jewry. Whether in combination with dry goods or tailoring, or conducted in a completely retail or the questionable wholesale-retail category, the clothing business in the 50's was open sesame to success. Many immigrant Jews brought to America a knowledge of and experience in the manufacture of clothing. Trained in the old country as tailors, they arrived in America at a time when ready made clothing was becoming popular. Until 1835 this trade was almost entirely confined to the furnishing of sailor sea outfits. Americans had been accustomed to having their clothes made at home by a seamstress or sewing slaves although the rich often employed a tailor. As families grew wealthier and traveled, and as tastes in fashions improved, the towns and villages were visited by professionals adept in cutting and fitting. In New York the arrival of many immigrants, with little time to wait for measurings and fittings before they could continue their westward journey, made it necessary that tailors keep on hand a large assortment of sizes and styles. Theodore Greisinger, writing in his *Lebende Bilder aus America*, claimed, "die ganze Schneiderzunst ist deutsch."[12] The appearance of the sewing machine at this time gave tremendous impetus to the industry. Invented by Elias Howe in 1845, improved by Singer in 1851, the machine could not only accomplish in one day what ten sewers could do by hand but was stronger, more regular and more durable.[13] The popularity of the sewing machine was attested by the presence in Nashville in

1860 of five agencies each of whom advertised a superior product ranging in prices from $60 to $150.[14]

From the census, business directories and newspapers, the names of nine Jewish tailors have been verified.[15] Of the three tailoring and clothing establishments, only that of M. Sulzbacher may be positively identified as Jewish. It was in the wholesale and retail clothing business that the largest number of Jews were engaged. Here they were to be found as both employer and employee.[16] The status of clerk was for those who were eager to push ahead of short duration.[17]

The dry goods and clothing stores were probably forerunners of the later department stores or small neighborhood shops that catered to all members of the family. There was little ready made clothing for women for whom these stores stocked parasols, sunshades, fans, gloves, hats, shoes, laces, embroideries and dress goods.[18]

The times, the personalities and the fashions were revealed in the advertisements of the 50's. As early as 1847 Louis Powers invited prospective customers to call and examine the merchandise at his Great Western Clothing Store on Market Street opposite Union Hall, where a large assortment of ready made clothing could be purchased "very low, for cash."[19] By supplying "every article required to adorn the outer man and make him an object of admiration to his friends,"[20] Mr. Powers demonstrated sound business acumen. His motto was, "not to be sold or undersold by any man or combination of men."[21] His establishment weathered competition for it was still flourishing at the same address in 1860 although the name had been changed to the Tennessee Clothing Depot. Louis Powers was a sincere believer in the South's cause as later events were to reveal. The following notice in a local paper, however, seemed to cloud any such patriotism with a suspicion of gathering in the shekels before it was too late:

Notes of City Bank and all solvent Banks in South Carolina, Georgia, Alabama and Kentucky taken at par. Nervous gentlemen who have lost confidence in state bonds and in the integrity of the

Union, now have an opportunity to deck themselves out in splendid style and calmly await the dissolution of the Union and the Day of Judgment. I also have $30,000 worth of property to dispose of on the same terms.

L. Powers
Tennessee Clothing Depot
34 Market Street opposite Union[22]

Mike Powers, brother of Louis, was equally successful in his clothing store housed for all of that decade at 11 Public Square. In spite of close personal ties, the brothers consistently advertised that their respective establishments had no connection with any other business house of the same name. In the 1859 business directory Mike was also listed as a partner in the Myers-Hunt carriage manufactory. The partner Myers may have been an uncle-in-law of Mike's and a son of the pre-Revolutionary Benjamin Myers discussed in chapter one. Myers-Hunt and company made carriages, barouches, buggies, trolling wagons, rockaways and sulkies.[23]

A third Powers brother, Sam, had been a member of the large and successful clothing house Milus Brothers and Company, in Cincinnati. In 1850 Sam and a friend formed a new business known as Powers and Johnson.[24] Upon the failure of this venture Sam came to Nashville and he was listed as a salesman for Louis Powers for the years 1855-60.

William Milius, another member of the aforementioned Cincinnati concern, Milius Brothers and Company, also arrived in Nashville early in the decade. He formed with Elias Wolf, who was already established here, a wholesale and retail clothing store at the corner of Market Street and the Public Square. Their advertisement stressed that goods were expressly made for them.[25]

Morris Cohn operated the City Clothing Store on North Market Street which had been purchased in 1849 from J. B. Nichol.[26] The editor of the *Gazette* personally vouched for the excellence of Mr. Cohn's merchandise. The motto of this house was "small profits, quick returns."[27]

Martin Sulzbacher arrived in Nashville in 1851 after a short sojourn in Pulaski which followed a residence of about ten years in Cincinnati. The City Clothing Store was sold in 1853 to Sulzbacher; and Cohn, its former owner and step brother of Sulzbacher, was off to make his fortune in the West. The new owner supplied everything necessary in a gentleman's furnishing house including Spanish cloaks, silk and satin plush vests, cravats, valises and carpet bags.[28] For an advertisement in the *Republican Banner,* Mr. Sulzbacher was awarded the editor's comments that acclaimed him "a man of probity and urbanity" and entitled to a large share of patronage.[29] Mr. Sulzbacher consistently reminded the public that his cutter Pfeiffer, was always on hand to assure a beautiful fit.

Personal selection of merchandise in eastern cities by the junior member of the firm was the advertising gimmick of Lande and Elsbach.[30] Aaron Lande's enterprises pre-dated the chain store era. In addition to a cap manufactory established in the 1840's, he was a partner in two clothing establishments, the Lande-Elsbach Store on North Market Street and the Lande-Schlessinger store on the Public Square.[31]

The dry goods merchants were probably small operators as they did a minimum of advertising of their Parisian plaids, French Merinos, embroidered shawls and mourning goods. Among the most financially successful was Isaac Stein[32] whose store at 12 Union Street was established in the early 50's. At the outbreak of the Civil War the Stein family returned to Germany, but a son, Joseph, born in Nashville in 1859, was to return to the city of his birth some thirty years later to become one of its leading citizens and merchants.[33]

As the first public buildings in Nashville were situated on the Public Square, it resulted naturally that business houses were established near by. The Square was also the headquarters for the farmer who brought in produce to exchange for staples. By 1860 the commercial district extended from the Public Square and Cedar Street on the north to Broad Street on the south, and from Front Street on the east to Summer Street on the west. The intervening streets, running east and west, were Deaderick,

Union and Spring which was in the process of name changing to Church Street. Spring Street divided the city into north and south, as every street crossing it began with number one north and number one south. The streets extending north and south were Front, Market, College, Cherry and Summer.

By 1860 the public square was being taken over by wholesale establishments; thirteen of the twenty-eight business houses were engaged in the wholesale trade.[34] The popular retail section was on College and Union Streets. As early as 1857 it became evident that the crowding of wagons and drays around the Public Square was pushing the retail business westward.[35] Actually no street was devoted exclusively to any one business industry. North Cherry housed many dentists, doctors and attorneys; College near Union attracted the banks; and on South Market, South College and Broad Streets the wholesale groceries were located. The majority of the clothing and dry goods stores, owned by Jewish merchants, were concentrated on Broad and North and South Market.

Nashville's Front Street, along the Cumberland River, had an undesirable section with a number of saloons and brothels.[36] Two businesses conducted by Jews were situated on Front Street. One was a small clothing store located at 20 South Front and owned by S. Levick. However, by 1860 Mr. Levick had moved his business to Broad near College. The second business house, a variety and commission house, was owned and operated by Isaac Joseph whose bizarre ideas of advertising were not only unique but noisy. In addition to the beat of the drum which Mr. Joseph termed the St. Louis and New Orleans custom of calling the buyers together, a large bell was suspended from an upper window and it would clang with great violence to attract people to the auctions.[37]

A local auction sale was described by Mrs. Sam Cowell, wife of an English actor, when she and her husband toured Nashville in May 1960 as follows:

> . . . for the last three evenings an auction had been going on in a store facing us, to call people, to which a huge bell, which hangs

from an upper window, is clanged every now and then, with great violence. The articles sold consist of 'Bogus' jewellery, and it was at first amusing, but since has become painful to hear the auctioneer's glib falsehoods as to their value, etc.

He is very rapid in his utterance . . . 'Here gentlemen is a gold guard chain—15 pennyweights, and 8 grains in weight. 18 carat gold—the finest made. Such a chain as may be worn by a gentleman or worn by a lady when a gentleman has brought it to present to her.—Be kind enough to look at it gentlemen, you are not obliged to buy it because you look at it, although the very sight of such a beauty is worth a dollar alone. Neither too long nor too short. 25 rings in it, and all of pure gold, pure as your mother's wedding ring. Shall I say $30 for the chain, shall I say $30, shall I say $29, shall I say $28? Gentlemen, have you any idea of what the chance is you are throwing away. A chain like that on a gentleman's waistcoat is sufficient to prove that he is no loafer. Am I offered $20 for the chain . . . and so on till perhaps he begins at $2. Then he goes on 'I am offered $2 $2 $2 $2, two dollars and a ha'af shall have it. $2 $2 $2 $2 and a ha'af shall have it, and a ha'af, and a ha'af and a ha'af shall have—$2 and a quarter, and a quarter, and a ha'af shall have it.—15 pennyweights and ten grains in weight, pure gold, or I return the money from this till 12 o'clock at night—no advance upon $2 and a quarter—No advance? —gone! Now gentlemen, here is the watch I have been looking for all night. This is an English made, pure gold, silver-gilt watch, with a new kind of action which we call the patent revolver—How much for her gentlemen? If she goes at less than $60 she goes too cheap. Every man ought to have a watch—etc., etc.[38]

As early as 1851 Mr. Joseph advertised that he would receive all kinds of marketing in exchange for merchandise.[39] This system of bartering was common in the rural and isolated areas. Frederick Olmsted in his travels in the South in 1853-54 wrote of men who had never seen a dollar in their lives. Stores doing business with the farm area accepted crops in exchange for merchandise. This led to the establishment of commission houses that would either sell the crops in Nashville or forward them to eastern markets for sale there. Isaac Joseph's auction store was such a commission house. The letterhead of a local concern in 1848 listed the following articles that were bought and exchanged: wool, feathers, beeswax, ginseng, flax seed, hemp, bacon, lard, tallow, dried fruit, peach brandy, beans, peas, hides, furs and pelts.[40]

In addition to the commission houses that purchased from the farmer, there were purchasing agents who personally selected items for rural and urban customers. A local advertisement in 1857 announced the services of an agent for the purchase of any item from wearing apparel to furniture. The cost for such service was 5% commission on purchases of less than $100 or 2½% for those exceeding $100.[41]

The large business establishments purchased from eastern houses on long and generous credit arrangements, consequently they were able to extend to their customers credit on a twelve month basis. The neophyte Jewish merchants were content to sell cheaper for cash unconsciously accepting the sage advice of the nineteenth century business advisor, Freeman Hunt, who cautioned against the "pernicious system of credit." Mr. Hunt described credit as "hazardous trading for the sake of doing business."[42]

It is unlikely that the Jewish merchants of Nashville, the great majority of whom were struggling and unimportant shop owners, read either Freeman Hunt, editor of a national merchant magazine, or J. B. DeBow, the popular editor of a southern business journal. DeBow's Journal was highly recommended by the local press. The Nashville newspapers, numbering five dailies in 1860, served as the merchants primer. Three pages of the four page newspaper were devoted to advertisements. The local readers were convinced of the worth of the fifty cent charge for a six line insertion if one wanted to "rent a home, employ a clerk, mechanic or teacher, hire a servant, find a boarder, seek a position, report the loss or find of articles"[43] or, most important of all, to sell merchandise.

The 1857 city business directory celebrated the virtues of many of its advertisers in verse. Unfortunately none of the Jewish advertisers rated a rythmical notice. Hughes Brothers, distinguished artists, were publicized with:

The face and form of those you love
When they are gone to Heaven above,
Will soothe the heart of grief and sadness
As we gaze upon their beauteous likeness.[44]

The following metrical composition solicited trade and support for Nashville's wholesale houses:

Here may be found a splendid stock;
Why go to Boston or New York?
To order here your clothes are made
Why not support your Southern trade.[45]

The dentist who employed these couplets undoubtedly, we hope, was rewarded with patients:

O! to have good friends to leave us,
Such as sound white teeth have been,
Is to all most sad and grievous
Till the doctor puts them in again.[46]

The *Asmoneau,* a weekly Jewish paper also resorted to verse for its advertisers with:

If your face or hands are pimpled o'er
Or burnt with sun till they are sore
"Ballards medicated Toilet Soap"
Will brighten up your face with hope.

price 25¢[47]

A business category that attracted many Jewish immigrants in the latter half of the nineteenth and early twentieth centuries was that of shoemaker. But strangely few Jewish shoemakers were listed in the business directories of the fifties. In all likelihood there were some who were unable to pay the charge for an insertion of their name. S. Steinmeier was listed only in the 1853 directory. S. Cohn, boot and shoe manufacturer, appeared in both the 1855 and 1857 directories. Many of the boot and shoe concerns of this era sold trunks, valises, carpet bags and bonnet boxes.

In 1859 shoemaking was revolutionized by a machine, that

could sew soles and uppers together.[48] In early America the itinerant shoemaker would visit the homes and farms and there cut, peg and sew the leather into shoes for the family. However, this method did not guarantee the fit that a modern custom made shoe gives. Until 1880 few shoes were made specifically for the left and right foot. Lasts were straight and could be worn on either foot. Measurements were obtained by a string or stick, marking the length from heel to toe. Goodyear's process of vulcanization, patented in 1844, contributed further to changes in shoe manufacture as rubber shoes and rubber heels began to appear. The individual shoemaker was giving way to the shoe factory.

An ownership of a grocery had always attracted entries due in large measure to the small capital necessary. To the cracker, pickle and flour barrel stores, the young immigrant was drawn. He could rely on his German speaking friends and neighbors for support, encouraged by the realization that people like to trade with those who speak the same language.[49] The grocery store of the 50's dealt mainly in staples such as flour, sugar, lard, dried vegetables, parched coffee beans and molasses. For a "big nickel's worth" of bacon with a streak of lean, a streak of fat, not too lean and not too fat, the customer also requested the gift of a stick of candy. We may safely assume that bacon customers were not of the Jewish faith. For fresh meats, fruits and vegetables the man of the house usually made the purchases at the market house and farmer's market, which filled the Public Square from late evening until 10 A.M.[50] Scarcity of provisions, particularly in meats, led to a comment in the local press on the high price of chickens at twenty-five cents each.[51] David Elsbach was listed in the 1860 census as a dealer in produce.

Middle Tennessee was a large livestock area and it was a common sight to see herds of cattle being driven overland from Nashville to Cincinnati for slaughter. With no information on the Jewish cattle dealer, Sampson Laufer,[52] the modern reader may justifiably rely on his imagination for any description of the duties and problems involved in that field of endeavor.

One development of the 50's was that of large scale bakeries.

H. Spitz added to his bakery, on South Market Street below Broad, a confectionery which sold fruits, wines, preserves and catered for weddings and parties. Mike Shyer's confectionery store was located at 24 Broad Street. The delicacy, ice-cream, had just appeared on the local scene and met with immediate approval as shown in the opening of several ice-cream parlors. Eating places were often called saloons as evidenced in the advertisements in the 1860 business directory of a ladies' ice-cream saloon and a coffee and dining saloon.

Hotel living was quite common in the 50's. The fashionable hotel in Nashville was the St. Cloud at the corner of Spring and Summer Streets. Germans, having a reputation for cleanliness and good food, attracted travelers who felt safe and well fed in German hotels and boarding houses. Myer Lusky, an early Jewish settler in Nashville, after a career in fur trading which involved buying skins in America for shipment to Europe,[53] settled down in 1860 to operate a kosher boarding house at the busy corner of Broad and Cherry Streets.[54] Mr. Lusky's establishment boasted a large hall which was rented out for balls, dances and parties.[55]

Lager beer, scarcely known in America before 1850, attained great popularity in this decade. The scholar and clothing merchant, Henry Harris, had probably met with some reverses, for in 1860 he was a proprietor of a boarding house and saloon at 11 South College Street. Here Moses Bernstein worked as a saloon clerk.[56]

Perhaps the most extensive and important dispenser of wines and liquors was the establishment of Lyons and Company. The four Lyons brothers, Ben, Jacob, Lewis and Samuel, announced as early as July 1852 that they had handsomely fitted up a store at 19 Cedar Street, near the post-office and would sell cigars, tobacco, wines and liquors at both wholesale and retail.[57]

However, it was tobacco manufacturing that catapulted the Lyons into prominence. More and more capital was being invested in Nashville in this industry, first, because Nashville was near the source of the raw material, a fine quality tobacco that ranked among the best, and second, there was an ever growing

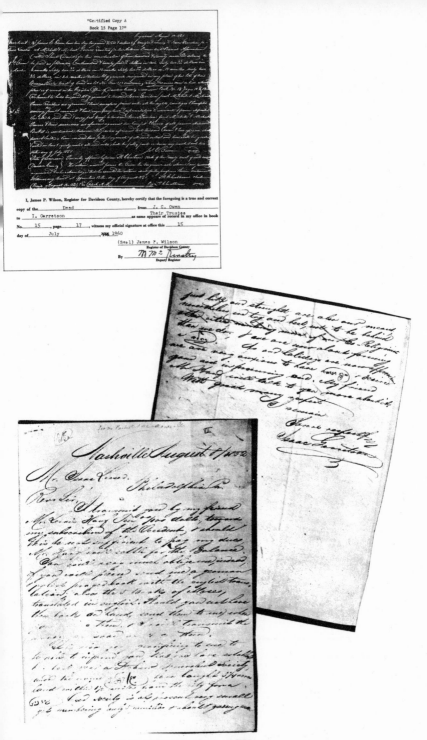

Above—Deed to Cemetery Property, 1861.
Below—Garritson's "Five Families and Eight Young Men" letter, 1852.

Advertisements in Business Directory 1853

Above—Meyer Lusky Passport, 1855.
Below—Lyons Brothers Advertisement, 1855.

Advertisements of Summer Resorts
1856

State of Tennessee, Davidson County—ss.

TO ANY REGULAR MINISTER OF THE GOSPEL, HAVING THE CARE OF SOULS, OR TO ANY JUSTICE OF THE PEACE.

These are to authorize you, or either of you, to solemnize the Rites of Matrimony between Nathan Cline and Emma Laufer of our County, agreeably to the direction of an Act of Assembly in such case made and provided; Provided Always, That the said Emma Laufer ... be an actual resident in this County; otherwise these shall be null and void, and shall not be accounted any license or authority to you, or either of you, for the purpose aforesaid, now than though the same had never been prayed or granted; &c.

Given at the Clerk's Office of said County Court, this 27th day of June 1857.

F. R. Cheatham ... Clerk of Davidson County Court.
By B. R. Cheatham D C.

NASHVILLE HIGH SCHOOL.

Report for four weeks ending May 27, 1857, of the SCHOLARSHIP, DEPORTMENT and ATTENDANCE of Miss M. L. Thomas

STUDIES PURSUED. J. Thomas.

Obtained in	Latin.	Greek.	French.	Geometry.	Algebra.	Philosophy.	Physiology.	Rhetoric.	Arithmetic.	Grammar.	Geography.	Spelling.	Composition.	Declamation.	General Average in Recitations.
			170			171 179	182		189						177.2 marks

Note.—Correct standard of Recitations, - 200 marks. Deportment, - 100 " Attendance, - 100 "
Note.—The Parent or Guardian is requested to examine, sign, and return this Report by the Pupil.

J. F. PEARL, Superintendent.

Obtained for Deportment, - 95 marks. Absent from School, - 0 days. Late at School, - 0 times. Left School before its close, -

Emily H. Brown, Teacher.
S. T. Penney, Teacher in English.

R. D. BLUM ENGRAVER & PRINTER, CEDAR STREET 18, NASHVILLE!

Takes great pleasure in informing his friends and the Public generally, that he is prepared to do

Plain and Ornamental Engraving,

Die Sinking and Embossed Printing,

ADDRESS ENVELOPES,

BUSINESS CARDS

Printed with neatness and dispatch, Seals of every description neatly Engraved and presses furnished, Steel Stamps for Silversmiths, Blacksmiths, etc. Also, Stencils' Brands, Marking Plates for Linen, Door Plates, etc., all kinds of patterns for Embroidery, Engraved to order at shortest notice.

Above—Cline-Laufer Marriage
License, 1857.
Center—A High School Report, 1857.
Below—R. D. Blum Advertisement, 1859.

Left—Lottery Advertisements, 1856.
Right—Railroad and Stage Coach Schedules, 18

Above—Jacob Ellis Naturalization Record, 1860.
Below—Union Street between Cherry and Market, 1860.

Mr. M. Elsbach at Nashville Tenn.
Peoria Illinois March 27. 1862

Dear Sir!

As I have the intention to become a Candidate for the office your laudable Congregation advertized for in the Israelite, I beg your leave to ask your kind information in regard to certain points connected with that position, as a preliminary prelude to my sending to you my petition.

How long ago is your Congregation organized, and by what charter is it recognized by the Legislature of your state, by a general or by a special Charter? —

How many children are there to be instructed in the congregational school, how many hours daily, how many days weekly, and what arrangement did your Congregation make in regard to the time of instruction during the hot season? —

Which of the three customs [מנהגים] have you adopted in your Synagogue; the German, Polonian, or American? —

Which sources of income could be counted as pertaining to the perquisites of your Hazan, Shohet, Teacher & Mohel? —

Is there any prospect now, that the salary of that officer, in case he should succeed to satisfy your laudable Congregation, or at least a majority of the same, in the first year, would somewhat

Above left—Rabbi Rosenfeld Letter, 1862.
Above right—Front page of Redelsheimer Prayer Book.
Below—View of Nashville, 1862.

Above—The Lande children. Below—The Dorothy Sulzbacher Sampler.

Above—Mr. and Mrs. Martin Sulzbacher.
Below—Mr. and Mrs. Henry Spitz.

market for tobacco products. The Lyons boys recognized the potential in this home industry and in 1857 they enlarged their establishment, invested more capital and found themselves in a really big business venture. They met with immediate success. In spite of their enlarged force they were unable to fill the orders.[58]

Cigarettes were not yet in use; there was much pipe smoking and an even greater number of cigar smokers. The local press claimed Nashville enjoyed a larger trade in cigars than any other city of the same size in the country.[59] Although the 50's saw the beginning of the commercial manufacture of chewing gum, it had little impact upon the popularity of tobacco chewing or snuff dipping, a common practice among women of the lower classes. Foreign visitors were always offended at the frequency of expectoration that accompanied an inexhaustible supply of saliva. No place was safe from the nauseating tobacco stain in spite of the ubiquitous spittoons.

The sign of a tobacco shop was the life sized figure of an Indian warrior or warrior's wife which stood outside the shop. Mr. L. D. Goldberg opened a tobacco establishment on Cedar Street in 1855 about the same time that a similar shop owned by the Messers Bloomstein and Markowiecz opened on North Cherry Street.[60]

The excellence of the cigars made and sold in Nashville was attested by the honors won at the first annual exhibition of the Mechanics Institute of Tennessee, the first exhibition of its kind in the state. At the Odd Fellows Hall in October 1855, Bloomstein and Markowiecz received a diploma and Messers Lyons and Company honorable mention for fine tobacco and cigars.[61] The third exhibition of the Institute was combined with the first State Fair in 1857 and was held at the newly acquired State Fair grounds. Once again Lyons and Company won a diploma for Tennessee cigars and Virginia and North Carolina tobacco.[62]

Although the inhabitants of agricultural Tennessee had an "indifferent attitude toward industry,"[63] there had been movements in the state to encourage manufacturers. As early as 1842 J. Gray Smith published in London a brief tract describing in extravagant language the profits that would accrue to capital and labor upon migration to East Tennessee.[64] The advantages of cheap labor, nearness to raw materials and nominally priced investment property were the premises of an appeal by E. Steadman in 1851 for investment in and development of manufacturing in the South.[65] As early as 1847 the leading business men of Nashville had formed a Board of Trade[66] but their real concern was the advancement of Nashville's trade in cotton, tobacco, flour and grain. A spirit of community cooperation was evident in 1856 in the signatures of leading business men for the selection for a site for a proposed new bridge. E. Franklin and Jacob Bloomstein were among the petitioners.[67] In a small measure the Mechanics Institute and the State Fair exhibitions had publicized the advantages of manufacturing.

Actually, the most successful job of selling the industrial spirit in Tennessee to Tennesseans was done by the articulate newspapers. They were the promulgators of the virtues to be found in the hum of the shuttle, the rattle of machinery and the shriek of the steam whistle.[68] Editorials appealed for lowered rents and the increased building of small homes to attract the low income group. The legislature was petitioned to make internal improvements to meet the progress being made in the North; the merits of railway extension were pleaded. The successes of those who had embarked upon such business ventures were cited in an attempt to awaken Nashville to a realization that manufacturing was a means to retain wealth in and promote progress for the community.[69]

By 1859 the city trade was valued at ten times the manufactures.[70] In addition to Lyons and Company, manufacturers of cigars, and Myers, Hunt and Company, carriage and coach makers, there were at least two Jewish immigrants who advertised as manufacturers. M. Cohn, for part of the decade, was a maker of pens, pencils and ink. As early as 1849 Aaron Lande advertised a cap manufactory on Market Street where men's, ladies and children's caps were made to order in any size and of a variety of materials.[71] David Elsbach was a member of this concern for part of the 50's as the concern kept pace with the "principal hatters in the East." In the early 60's Aaron was joined by his brother Nathan who had conducted a business in Shelbyville, Tennessee, in the 50's.

A fondness for jewelry was characteristic of both men and women in the nineteenth century. The men's waistcoats were fastened with jewelled buttons; fancy studs and scarf pins complemented their attire. The women adorned themselves with bracelets, rings and brooches. At an early age the ears of the girls were pierced for a lifetime of adorned ear lobes. The jewelry business was given an extensive boost by the production of the first factory-made watch in 1850. I. W. Sobel and brother D. L. advertised as not only watchmakers but jewelers and importers, both retail and wholesale. Other jewellers and watchmakers were S. H. Coleman, H. Cohen and S. Marcus.[72]

Undoubtedly, Nashville Jewry's greatest artist of this period was the engraver, R. D. Blum, whose beautiful work adorned the ark of the congregation, Mogen David. Blum, a maker of jewelry, was particularly adept in metals including silver, gold, brass, iron and untempered steel. To his establishment, first located on Deaderick Street and later on Cedar, he attracted customers for any type of seal which included those of Masons, Odd Fellows, Sons of Temperance and public officials.[73] The brothers J. and L. Swartzenberg were listed in 1860 census as dealers in metals.

Nashville, in 1854, became the first Southern city to adopt a plan for public education. There had existed public state schools known as common schools against which there existed much prejudice. Many objected to education at public expense and the wealthy preferred the education of their children at private institutions. The field of education was limited and restrictive. A local Jewish resident did, however, teach languages in a Female Seminary at Mt. Sterling, Kentucky, in the 1840's. He was Julius Ochs whose European education had given him a mastery of French, Italian, Spanish, Hebrew, German and English.[74] No religious identification has been available for either the Hungarian lawyer and linquist, Alexander Kocsiss, who offered his services as a teacher of Hungarian, Latin, Greek, German,

Italian and French[75] or for the Polish musicians Louis Levinski and Julius Losminski.[76]

Judah Frankland was a journalist on the Nashville *Daily Gazette* at the time of his death in 1866. He had, however, established himself as a writer prior to his service in the Confederate Army.[77]

In this decade of repeated epidemics, the masses placed great faith in homeopathic colleges, Indian doctors, medicinal herbs and patent medicines. The legal requirements for the status of doctor were three years of study with a practicing physician and two courses of lectures at a medical college.[78] No city or state Boards of Health had been established.

A card which read J. Mitchell, Indian doctor, was placed among the doctor's cards in the first Nashville business directory of 1853. This medicine man, a signer of the deed to the first Jewish cemetery property, was referred to as Doctor by A. E. Frankland, an early writer of Jewish congregational history. All available information confirms this writer's suspicions that the Indian doctor was the same Jacob Mitchell who in the 1840's operated a stage coach line from Little Rock to Hot Springs where he owned and managed a hotel from 1846 to 1849. His hotel, opened all year, advertised its good food in both the *Arkansas Gazette* of Little Rock and the *Daily Picayune* of New Orleans. A letter, dated July 10, 1848, and written by a person known only as "Bally," commented on the Jewish faith of the landlord of the Hot Springs Hotel adding further that his knowledge of herbs and their use had gained for him the title of doctor.[79] The Nashville *Gazette* for July 7, 1852, stated that Dr. Mitchell was an Indian botanical doctor who rejected the use of medicines favored by the medical faculty. With his preparations of roots and herbs he followed the treatment commonly practiced by both the North American Indian and the pioneers of the South and West. Dr. Mitchell treated patients at his office on Market Street near the Public Square and at his infirmary on the corner of Vine and Demonbreun Streets. A crumbling tombstone in the Nashville Jewish cemetery inscribed "Jakos Mitchell —died 1859" is probably the final link in the life chain of one

Jacob Mitchell who in the 1830's with his brothers, Hyman and Levy, were the earliest Jewish settlers of Little Rock, Arkansas.[80]

Dr. S. Marcus who had been a practicing physician in Cincinnati arrived in Nashville in 1856 and advertised himself as a surgeon and occulist. He not only had sworn affidavits to authenticate his claims for the correction of cross eyes but he modestly announced that he could cure every disease of the eye.[81]

Nashville's most prominent Jewish doctor of this area was Gustavus Schiff, a native of Germany and a graduate of the University of Wuersburg. Schiff arrived in this country in 1857 and settled first in Murfreesboro where relatives were already established. In a local paper in 1861, he advertised that he had studied five years at colleges in Berlin, Wuersburg, Prague and Vienna and was now offering his services as a physician, surgeon and accoucheur to the people of Nashville and vicinity. His office at 28 Cherry Street was in the neighborhood popularized by doctor's offices.[82]

An announcement that Doctor S. Levy had his office at his home on North Summer Street is all we know of this physician.[83]

The pharmacist was called an apothecary in 1852 when the American Pharmaceutical Association was founded. There was a pressing need for the code of ethics which it adopted. The newspapers advertised the restorative qualities of patent medicines with signed testimonials. Hailed as the saviors of womankind, these remedies cured everything from toothache, which was often called dental neuralgia, to club feet. A forerunner of the twentieth century psychiatrist was evident in the fabulous claims of Dr. Morse's Invigorating Cordial. It was the only sure and safe remedy for general debility and nervous affliction. It could remove depression, excitement, dislike of society, incapacity for study or loss of memory.[84] Equally exaggerated were the claims of a locally manufactured vegetable extract, Cherokee Remedy. "It is an article of more real value than the gold mines of California; it never fails to cure all diseases of the urinary organs in less time and with less trouble than any other known article."[85]

The German traveler, I. J. Benjamin, viewed with horror the

deception and quackery practiced in America. He wrote, "Remedies considered in Europe with awe are administered by Americans with boldness."[86] The indiscriminate use of laudanum and paregoric in illnesses of children undoubtedly killed many.

A small number of Jews, mostly peddlers, very likely participated in the sales of patent medicines. Lyons and Company, the prominent cigar manufacturers, wine and liquor dispensers, were agents for Dr. Mills Bitters, Hostetters Stomach Bitters and Green's Aromatic Sarsaparilla. Their medicated brandy was especially recommended as a preventive and cure for diseases of the bowels.[87]

Repeatedly spiritualists, phrenologists and fortune tellers have deceived the gullible by their practice of divination. In nineteenth century America, humbugs and charlatans basked in the sunshine. Women were particularly gullible in the purchase of magic powders to charm men of their choice. Certainly, Mr. Louis Ullman, of Columbia, Tennessee, must not be categorized as a faker but the psychic powers possessed by his weather-indicator are questionable. Mr. Ullman was the discoverer of an oriental talisman that was made from an indestructible plant of the Arabian desert. This magic stick could foretell the weather from twenty-four to forty-eight hours in advance. A testimonial of the value of this weather forecaster was given by a professor of medicine at the University of Nashville.[88] Such approval by an illustrious person, undoubtedly, sold many of these rain indicators at one dollar each.

In this prosperous decade, the country, businesswise and industrywise, experienced phenomenal growth and success. Half of the corporations, established between the years 1800 and 1860, were founded in this one decade.[89] The capital invested in manufacturing alone almost doubled in this ten year span.[90] This golden age of inventions and discoveries produced the McCormick reaper, the Otis elevator, the Colt revolver, the Singer sewing machine, vulcanization and kerosene. Nashville along with the rest of the country was tasting the sweet fruits of prosperity; her rise to prominence as a trade center was reflected in the erection of two bridges over the Cumberland

River, the building of new schools, new business houses and private dwellings. But the impetus given to commerce and internal improvements by the discovery of gold in California, and through the acquisition of vast western lands, led to over-expansion of industry, particularly of the railroads. This reached a breaking point in 1857 that paralyzed the large eastern cities. As factories closed and unemployment grew, repercussions were felt in the South especially in the tobacco area. Many Nashville merchants had difficulties trying to meet payments that were due. For first rate signatures to loans, other than banks, a local paper commented as early as 1855 that the rate of interest was 15 to 24% per annum and second class papers were available at an even higher rate.[91] In September 1857 there was a run on the Bank of Nashville that caused the bank to close for a short period, but the bank was solvent, and its assets were ample to meet all demands.[92] No banks failed in Nashville. From another section of Tennessee a merchant wrote to a New York creditor early in 1858:

> The money market is very tite [sic] The banks are not discount-ing and the planters have not sold their crops and it is almost impossible to get money. I have been merchandising in this place for 18 years and I have never seen anything like it before.[93]

Prices began to decline. Sugar that had been twelve and thir-teen cents a pound was now six cents.[94] The hard times fell heaviest on the small business man. Following the recession of 1857, vocational changes were noted for Louis and Jacob Bloom-stein, Henry Harris, Martin Sulzbacher and the Lyon Brothers.

The successful firm established by the four Lyons brothers was out of business when the 1859 business directory went to press, for only Lewis Lyons was listed in the cigar busi-ness. By then, Ben was operating a billiard hall on Union Street over York's Book Store. Both billiards and bowling were very popular games among all classes and the special Monday Ladies' Day[95] gave evidence that it appealed to both sexes. Mr. Lyons gained much patronage from exhibitions of well-known billiard players who would be brought to Nashville to delight local lovers of the game.[96] The business undoubtedly prospered for in June 1860 Mr. Lyons announced the opening of the Jenny Lind saloon adjacent to the billiard rooms. Lyons was personally acquainted with many of the theatrical folks and frequently donated to benefit performances in their honor. Mrs. Sam Cowell revealed in her diary in May 1860 a shocking bit of information concerning Ben Lyons:

> Pawn-broking is illegal here, but Sam took his father's watch and his gold medal to Mr. Lyons of the billiard rooms, who lent him $50.[97]

The following year the billiard hall had a new owner, Lewis Lyons, and a new name, "Rock City Billiard Saloon." Mr. Lyons employed twentieth century advertising tactics of attracting customers with handsome free gifts.[98]

The immigrant merchants often unintentionally violated the city ordinances because of alien habits and unfamiliarity with the language. The records of business suits, prosecuted in the circuit and criminal courts, reveal that the great majority of these cases were concerned with violation of the Sabbath, licensing and tippling. The litigation against Lande, Elsbach and Garritson by the Bank of Commerce dragged through the Chancery Court for eight years. The case merits our attention because of one aspect, the reason given by Mr. Garritson for failure to pay an apparently just claim against him.

In May 1858 the Bank of Commerce won a judgment against Aaron Lande and David Elsbach for $846, but at the time no property was found among the defendants to pay the judgments. Later the Bank instituted another suit claiming that in May 1857 Lande and Elsbach had deeded goods in their storehouse on the Public Square, notes, and accounts due them, to Isaac Garritson who was to pay all debts that had been incurred by Lande and Elsbach. The trustee, Garritson, did pay all the debts except that of the complainant, the Bank of Commerce. This debt he would not pay as he claimed that the bank had embraced usury. Finally, in December 1866 after the original suit and answers had been complicated by cross suits and the death of the defendant, Isaac Garritson, the court decided that there had been no proof of usury and the Garritson administrators were ordered to pay the augmented sum of $1296.51 to the Bank of Commerce.[99]

And so in that fertile vineyard which was to yield a rich harvest, the inhabitants of antebellum Nashville, native and foreign, Christian and Jew, planted their own small seed.

CHAPTER V

A Time to Speak

T HIS was a decade of harsh words. The problems of sectional controversies were not to be settled by compromising legislation. Instead, clashing personalities and differing political party philosophies combined to flame the passions of men into an explosion that was to tear the Union apart. In such a tense atmosphere, the naive Jewish immigrant, inexperienced and uninitiated in the responsibilities and privileges of government, was introduced to democratic procedures.[1]

When the Nashville convention met in June 1850 to unify Southern reaction to the compromise bill then before the Congress, there probably existed among the 7,629 Nashville white residents[2] less than a dozen Jews who were qualified voters of Davidson County.[3] However, the many applications for citizenship in the Criminal and Circuit Court records for this decade, are proof of the desire of the immigrant to assume his role as a responsible American citizen as soon as the five year residence requirement could be met.[4] But the great majority remained for a large part of the decade silent but observant witnesses to some of the bitterest and hardest fought contests for economic and political supremacy that the country had ever known.

Although restricted in active political participation, there was no legislation that forbade the immigrant from holding personal opinions. Since no one lived in a vacuum, it was inevitable that as men listened to or read about the subjects of states rights, slavery, abolition and temperance, they made personal decisions and arrived at their own convictions. And having political beliefs was as essential in this decade as life and death.

Foreign visitors were impressed with both the importance that Americans attached to every political issue and the great pleasure that they apparently derived from just talking about the govern-

ment.[5] Pre-election debates and rallies had more than political
significance. They offered a diversified and inexpensive means
of entertainment.[6] In addition to lengthy and often brilliant
oratory, the viewers were treated to the martial music of parades
with banners flying, to free dancing and free food. The immigrant was particularly impressed with the popular Fourth of
July celebration. In 1857 this event marked the first participation
in Nashville of the foreign citizens.[7] To the usual speeches and
dancing was added the fun of rifle shooting and the pleasure
of lager beer. The Germans organized a non-political military
group known as the German Yaegers in 1858[8], and for several
years their superior marching and wheeling heightened the
interest in these annual Independence Day celebrations.[9]

In 1850 there were in the country thousands of newspapers
and periodicals[10] that exerted a powerful influence on public
opinion. Unquestionably, much of the tension and conflict of this
era can be traced to the editorials that crusaded for and against
public land, public education, national powers, slavery, abolition,
women's rights, state's rights and more humane treatment of the
criminal and the insane. It was the time to talk, and the newspapers were articulate and convincing at every level from local
to international. The five daily papers were often abusive in
language as they campaigned for their candidates and parties
threatening their readers with predictions of disaster if they dare
fall prey to differing platforms.[11]

The municipal and county elections had not achieved the
political significance of their modern counterparts and in consequence merited little more than a declaration of known candidates and the final results of the elections. It is entirely within
the realm of reason to conclude that few if any Jews voted in
the annual municipal contests. Scheduled on the last Saturday
in September they were frowned on by observant Jews, who
were bound by the Biblical injunction to remember the Sabbath
and keep it holy. The county elections for sheriff, magistrate,
constable and the several court clerks were held on the last
Saturday in March. The local papers reported the unsuccessful
bid for constable from the city district in March 1861 of one

J. T. Lyons. The modern researcher can only ponder his relationship to the prominent tobacco manufacturers, the Lyons Brothers one of whom was named Jacob.

Prior to 1858 the affairs of the city were administered by a Mayor and a Board of sixteen Aldermen composed of two men elected from each of the eight wards. Until the incorporation of South Nashville into the city in 1854 there had been only six wards. In the last two years of the decade two Boards, a Board of eight Aldermen, one from each ward, and a Board of Councilmen, two from each ward, divided the municipal responsibilities. However, they met in joint conference on many of the local problems. The newspapers regularly printed the meetings of the City Council and Board of Aldermen and everyone could read of the decisions these men must make in matters as vastly different as passing on a petition for the erection of a frame house to the selection of a site for a new public school.[12]

Warnings to the naturalized citizen appeared regularly as the election day neared. The six months county residence requirement for voting often brought forth much quibbling at the polls. The new citizens were advised to take along their naturalization papers or some proof of citizenship.[13]

Although women had not been granted the franchise, their influence was apparent. A local paper sought their assistance in the election of its favorite candidates in the following appeal:

> Ladies of Tennessee, like the noble women of the Revolution who moulded bullets for their fathers, brothers and husbands to defend their homes, you can prepare Union tickets for the ballot boxes on the morning of the election—clip the ticket from the paper, fold and place in your sweetheart's watch-fob and bid them do their duty like men.[14]

The press manifested considerable interest in the filibustering adventures of the "gray-eyed man of destiny," William Walker. This native of Nashville, in 1856, set himself up as dictator of the Central American country of Honduras. The dictatorship was short-lived, however, as Walker was expelled in the following year. He returned to this country for a few months during which time he made a visit to friends in Nashville. Undoubtedly, any support of dictators and oppression must have been bewildering to the European immigrants who had hoped to find in this new world liberty and justice for all.

A striking example of the power of the printed word was demonstrated in the immediate popularity and acclaim that was given Harriett Beecher Stowe's *Uncle Tom's Cabin* or *Life Among the Lowly.* This story was first printed in June 1851 as a thirty-six issue serial in the Washington anti-slavery newspaper, *The National Era.* It created such a political stir that by mid 1853 over one million copies had been published. It was not only credited with attracting millions to the Abolitionists but with sowing the seeds of the Civil War.

Of the eighty-three papers published in Tennessee, sixty-six were political.[15] The five Nashville dailies were in this category.[16] Although they bitterly opposed one another in political campaigns, they found unanimity on many of the national issues. They believed in the preservation of the Union in spite of sincere convictions that each state retained those powers not spelled out in the constitution. The papers also supported the institution of slavery. As the press hammered at these problems and the candidates orated and argued, the immigrant listened and learned the elementary course in how to act and behave as an American.

The antebellum press headlined the explosive temperance question. This story of the bottle and the pledge, which in the 1840's had been largely a moral war against drinking, became in the 1850's a weighty influence in politics. The movement gained stimulus in 1854 with Timothy Arthur Shay's *Ten Nights in a Bar Room and What I Saw There.* By 1860 one million copies of this literary effort had been published. The country was swept by a fervent enthusiasm for prohibition. The prominent temperance leaders, Lyman Beecher, Neal Dow and John Gaugh, inspired bands of reformed drunkards to travel from one mass meeting to another exhorting men to take the pledge. On the evil drink was placed the blame for waste, crime, ignorance, pauperism and shattered health. In Tennessee the first statewide prohibition law had been passed in 1838 but was repealed eight years later. Now that the problem had entered the political arena, more and more schemes were invented to get it on the statute books. All during the 1853 session of the State Legislature the issue turned up, and in one day thirty petitions were entered on this one subject.[17]

In the gubernatorial campaign of 1855 prohibition became one of the main issues. The temperance committee placed before the two candidates Meredith Gentry and Andrew Johnson, two questions: (1) Are you in favor of a law prohibiting the sale of intoxicating liquors as a beverage? (2) Will you if elected recommend in your message to the legislature passage of such a law at an early period in the session? Gentry's reply indicating opposition to tippling and Johnson's admission of his disapproval of the Maine liquor law, fell short of the demands of the committee and so it set about to seek its own candidate.[18]

The German papers in this country attacked total abstinence; consequently, Germans came in for more than their share of criticism. The establishment of temperance societies received little or no support from Jews. They could not comprehend the need of an organization to indoctrinate them in virtues of temperance. The life of the orthodox Jew was circumscribed by the Biblicial injunctions of moderation in all things as the best security against overindulgence. In 1859 Rabbi J. J. Peres of Memphis explained the Jewish stand on temperance in these words—"To give one's self over to the abstinence of a covenant, or to live like a hermit, or to renounce all enjoyment is a sin against which, it is wisdom to guard ourselves."[19]

The question of slavery and its extension into the recently acquired territories were definitely the paramount issues of the fifties. Beginning with the compromise of 1850 a series of legislative acts, including the Kansas-Nebraska Act and the Dred-Scott Decision, kept the matter bubbling and exploding. Events in bleeding Kansas and John Brown's raid at Harper's Ferry, Virginia, added fuel to an already blazing fire. The concern within the state was a natural one as one-third of the wealth of the state was the investment of 111 million dollars in 275,000 slaves.[20]

In 1859 sixteen bills on the Negro question were introduced in the State Legislature.[21] This had been preceded by months of heated debate and argument on the question of expelling the 7,000 free blacks from the state. Nashville's slaves were valued as taxable property in 1856 at over one million dollars.[22] However, the local legislation on slaves and free blacks was more in the category of protection and restriction. In the fall of 1857 a bill was introduced in the Council of Aldermen to permit slaves and free blacks the privilege of passing unmolested, on promise of good behavior, from sun down to nine o'clock and to hold public worship under the supervision of some discreet white person.[23] However, a petition from two colored men to have a "ball" was rejected on grounds that it was contrary to law.[24] The few abolitionists in the state were confined almost entirely to East Tennessee.[25] In middle Tennessee public opinion was definitely favorable to slavery.

There was no national organization that spoke in the name of American Jewry. Although the national Jewish periodicals successfully sidetracked the issue of slavery, many prominent religious leaders did not remain quiet and were to be found on both sides of the question voicing their approval. The American and Foreign Anti-Slavery Society reported in 1853 that the Jew had taken no steps for or against slavery.[26]

Nationally the great majority of Germans opposed the institution of slavery, but on the local scene, it would seem, they maintained an impersonal attitude toward it. Seven of the 3,226 slaves in Nashville in 1860 were owned by seven Jews.[27]

There was one known local defender of slavery. He was Rabbi Samuel Raphael whom the *Republican Banner* called an "eloquent and learned minister of the Israelites of this city." Dr. Raphael in a letter to his son, which was published in the local press, attempted to defend slavery by quoting Biblical passages which condoned the practice.[28] To date there is no further evidence that local Jewry participated in the "half-free—half-slave" controversy.

At the beginning of the decade Tennessee was about equally divided between the two national political parties, the Whigs and the Democrats. The division between the parties was not always clear. Neither party was sectional, each was to be found in every state and in each party there were warring factions on many of the national issues. In Tennessee the majority in each of the parties were of the opinion that slavery was sanctioned by the constitution.

On the equally explosive issue of state's rights the two parties concurred in the belief that those powers not specified in the Constitution as belonging to the Federal government were to be regulated and administered by the states. The question of state's rights, undoubtedly, was an involvement in politics which aroused little response in the uninformed immigrant.

Without benefit of factual material it is safe to assume that the newcomer threw his support to the preservation of the Union. He had adopted the land because of its great promise of freedom and liberty to all. Certainly, as a new citizen who had recently sworn allegiance to his chosen country, he would be dedicated to protecting its democratic principles. The decision to remain within the Union, in preference to joining the seven Confederate States in February 1861, proves conclusively that the people of Tennessee desired the preservation of the Union.

It was a time of pointing fingers and accusing others of dividing the country.[29] The Whigs, later known as the American Party, condemned the Democrats for destroying the Union, and they in turn were labeled by the Democrats as Abolitionists. *The Union and American,* a dedicated organ of the Democratic Party, appealed for a united Southern vote for their candidate, John Breckenridge, by threatening a dissolution of the Union with the election of Lincoln.[30] A united South, but not a defiant South, answered the *Republican Banner* as they championed Tennessee's favorite son John Bell, a candidate for president on the Constitutional Union ticket.[31] In response to the support given by a New Orleans German paper to the Union Party of Bell and Everett, the local *Republican Banner* wrote: The German citizens are a reading and thinking people, so are for the defense of the Union."[32]

The new American was sensitive to anti-immigration propaganda. The South was, in the final analysis, more concerned with Southern interests than with being anti-foreign. Certainly the settlement of many newcomers in the free lands of the new territories had upset the sectional balance of power. Even in Tennessee there was a fear that immigration might strengthen the Abolition forces. Whether for this reason or for others, the fact remained that during the entire decade, not one governor mentioned or supported immigration in his message to the State General Assembly.[33] There were in the state in 1860, 21,226 inhabitants of foreign birth and in Davidson County, of the 31,056 white population, 4,382 were of foreign birth.[34]

It was out of a seething cauldron of nativism and religious bigotry that sputtered the fantastic stories of two Jewish memberships in the anti-foreign party known as the Know Nothing Party. This party came into existence in the early 1850's with the disintegration of the Whig Party. Since 1835 the Whigs had been the most influential party in Tennessee politics, but their power began to wane with the election of the last Whig governor in Tennessee, Governor William Campbell, who served from 1851-1853. The passage of the Kansas-Nebraska Act had split both the Whig Party and the Democratic Party. Anti-slavery factions in both formed a new party known as the Republican Party, but its influence was sectional and it never gained a foothold in the South. The splintered group of Whigs and Democrats who did not go into the Republican Party were drawn into the recently created American Party. This party was the outgrowth of nativist lodges that had banded together about 1850 under the name of the Order of the Star Spangled Banner. The order had gained such strength that by 1853 it emerged as a National political party known as the American Party or Know Nothing Party. It was called Know Nothing because the members responded to questions with "I know nothing." Due to the mystery and secrecy surrounding the order it attracted a large following. It was the first anti-foreign party in the country emphasizing the threat of aliens to American institutions. In many areas the foreign vote was beginning to be an important influence. The Know Nothings set out to exclude foreigners and particularly Catholics from holding office.

By 1854 there were about 100,000 members in Tennessee.[35] In the spring of that same year, the party appeared in Nashville and created quite a stir.[36] Numerous inquiries led to vague suppositions about the purposes and ceremonies of the mysterious order. To the delight of an inquisitive public, a seceder from the order divulged the secrets of indoctrination, which included nine baptisms in ice water.[37] Prior to this disclosure, Isaac Joseph had announced in the *Daily Gazette*, that he would enlighten those who would attend his sale of groceries, dry goods and sundries at his auction and commission house on Front Street.[38] Mr. Joseph's membership in an anti-foreign group is comprehensible when we realize that the gentleman was a native American, born in South Carolina.[39]

A careful study of the state and national election returns for the decade of the 50's revealed that Davidson County was the seat of a large and influential Whig following.[40] In all likelihood, many of these Whigs were drawn into the new party.[41] Its strength and popularity was evidenced in September 1854 when W. B. Shepard, on the morning of the city election, announced his candidacy for mayor and received 1,188 of the 1,471 votes that were cast for mayor.[42]

When the finger of suspicion was pointed at the National German Turnverein, as being dangerous to the welfare of the country, its national president answered with a statement of the purposes of the organization:

> It is an association of youth and men whose purpose is to invigorate the body, strengthen the mind, improve the health, promote social intercourse, have gymnastic exercise, debates, exchange opinions, promote singing groups . . . it is not an exclusive German society, it is open to all responsible people.[43]

The wave of nativism rolled on and in its billowy foam religion cast a cloudy spray. Protestant ministers joined the anti-Catholic forces, and one of their most forceful speakers was the East Tennessee editor of a Know Nothing paper, a former Methodist minister and a future state governor, William G. Brownlow.

The Jewish national magazines in protesting the intolerance of this nativist party, emphasized the Jewish teachings of equal justice and tolerance of all religions. The local papers defended the foreign and Catholic population, but the most forceful crusader of religious liberty was the *Nashville Union and American*. This democratic paper was naturally eager to expose all the weaknesses of its rival party.[44] Religious persecution and discrimination had been an endless problem for the Jew who had looked to his new adopted country as a land free of the guilt of man's inhumanity to man.

Whispers, rumors and condemnations continued as the new party attracted a multitude of followers. In the most bitterly contested gubernatorial race in Tennessee, the incumbent Andrew Johnson was running for reelection. Since membership in the Know Nothing Party was secret, no convention was held to select a candidate.[45] Meredith P. Gentry, in announcing his own candidacy, insisted he was a candidate of neither party but of the people of Tennessee.[46] The religious issue was recapitulated. A local paper upbraided any secret political organization that felt the necessity of curtailing the activities of only 1,400 Catholics with three churches in a state that could claim 624,295 Protestants with 2,011 churches.[47] Davidson County revealed its Whig leanings with a vote of 3,132 for Gentry against 1,783 for Johnson, the winner. The Know Nothing Party triumphantly swept the state and was able to control both Houses of the State Legislature with slight majorities.

The presidential campaign of 1856 between the Democratic nominee, James Buchanan and the American or Know Nothing nominee, Millard Fillmore, boiled over into a furiously feverish contest. A popular feature of this campaign was the organization of young men's clubs called Fillmore and Donelson clubs. The vice-presidential nominee on the Know Nothing ticket was Andrew Jackson Donelson, an adopted son of former President Andrew Jackson. Naturally there were a host of admirers and supporters for Tennessee's native son, and many of these issued an invitation through the newspapers to an organizational meeting of a Nashville Fillmore-Donelson Club. Among the list of

sponsors appeared the name of M. Sulzbacher.[48] The inclusion
of this name may have raised eyebrows, but the announcement
on the day following the organizational meeting that Mr. Sulzbacher had been elected one of the twelve vice-presidents was
overwhelming. The elevation of Mr. Sulzbacher, a foreigner, in
a group that thought "none but natives were to be put on guard"
was for the rival democratic paper, the *Union and American,* sur-
prising and confusing. Their astonishment was not only published
immediately but embellished with the comment that "Mr. Sulzbacher, a Jew, dealing in ready made clothing, might preside
with a great deal of dignity and may even be very capable
of keeping order when the dark lanterns assemble in the garretts
and cellars of the city."[49] Mr. Sulzbacher's forthright answer to
the slurs on his religion came quickly and unfaltering:

The *Union and American* seems to be very much vexed at the
idea that I, a foreign born citizen should withstand the specious
appeals of pseudo friends and prefer to serve my adopted country
in preference to following the dictates of passion and prejudice and
aid in placing in power those whose principles I have uniformly
condemned. The much vaunted democratic love of the foreigner
may gull those who have an eye to subsistence at the public crib,
or who fancy every attempt to check admitted evils, a blow at their
rights, but I feel that I have some interest in the future well being
of American republican institutions, and I prefer to act with that
party which does not seek to administer the government upon
principles to which as a Whig, I object. I am opposed on the one
hand, to the disunionists and antislavery meddlers of the free states;
and on the other, to that spirit in the democratic party which
could coerce the country into a sectional controversy, endangering
the rights of all, to achieve a mere party triumph; and regard the
election of Fillmore and Donelson, whose sound conservatism and
unionism, have been tried and approved, as the best thing to
restore the nation to repose and quiet. For these reasons, I
became a member of a Fillmore and Donelson club,—not strictly
an American organization—composed alike of Americans, Democrats and Whigs. If my fellow-citizens have thought proper to
place me in the position of an officer of the said club—a position
not of my seeking—I shall endeavor to prove by my conduct that

their confidence has not been misplaced. However, much it may comport with the *Union and American's* views of justice and propriety to cast a slur upon me for being a "Jew of this city, dealing in ready made clothing," I can say to it, that, decided as Jews have been, I am proud to belong to that race. Whatever may have been their sins, they have never, as Jews, interfered in the politics of the country, nor sought to make their religion the stepping stone to temporal power. Nor do the records of crime and pauperism bring up pyramids of evidence to reproach them of vice and degradation. If my humble calling as a "dealer in ready made clothing" is regarded as a badge of shame, the *Union and American* should show why it is so. I do not esteem it as such, any more than I do the trade of type setting which once employed the time of the editors of that paper or the trade of tailor which afforded Governor Johnson, in early life, the means to light his path to the high position of honor he has filled. My humble calling may furnish a foreigner and an unambitious Jew like me means to educate my American children and possibly, a son of mine may some day be quite as puissant a champion of liberty and democratic institutions as the editors of the *Union and American,* but I hope never so thoughtless or mistaken in his zeal as to disparage any one for his caste or his occupation.

In conclusion I would remark that if the *Union and American* did not mean to disparage me and my calling, I shall be much obliged to it for the gratuitous advertisement of my business; and shall not object if he keeps it up till the old Buck is slaughtered.

M. SULZBACHER[50]

So spoke Mr. Sulzbacher in defense of his religious and political convictions. The *Union and American's* "tongue-in-cheek" apology expressed no fault with Mr. Sulzbacher's religion or birthplace, but clearly branded the action of both the Know Nothing Party and Mr. Sulzbacher's acceptance of an office as hypocrisy.[51] The *Nashville Daily Gazette* and *The Israelite,* a national Jewish periodical, promptly joined the Sulzbacher supporters. The local paper, in the role of champion of the Jew, declared that by owning no allegiance to any foreign power the Jew remained faithful to his adopted country.[52] And Rabbi Isaac M. Wise, editor of *The Israelite,* cautioned that everyone follow his own convictions and slander not, ending with the statement that Mr. Sulzbacher had been more honorable than his opponent.[53]

Harsh words continued to augment the political agitation. On June 13, 1857, in Fayetteville, the two gubernatorial candidates Robert Hatton and Isham Harris, were debating their respective objectives. An altercation, over the use of the word infamous, resulted in Hatton being knocked from the platform. This was news and the press had a "field day."

Tension continued to mount and the clashes between the two Tennessee senators, John Bell and Andrew Johnson, only added to the turmoil. Eloquent and impassioned men were bringing their countrymen to the brink of a precipice. In the midst of this warfare of principles, it was difficult to think or act calmly. But the firing on Fort Sumter in April 1861, and Lincoln's subsequent call for troops from Tennessee dealt a blow to the pro-Union sentiments which had been expressed just two months earlier in a vote to remain in the Union. On June 8, 1861, the electorate went to the polls and expressed an overwhelming vote for separation. Tennesseans had cast their lot for a "divided house."

CHAPTER VI

A Time to Seek

W E are doing great work our fathers left undone—to secure education to high and low, rich and poor." So spoke Dr. W. K. Bowling on May 19, 1853, at the cornerstone setting for Nashville's first public school.[1] This was an era when education at public expense was unpopular and universally opposed. The average person in this country received during his lifetime only 434 days of schooling;[2] twenty-four and one-half per cent of the whites of Tennessee over twenty-one were illiterate.[3] It was evident that emphasis had not been placed on education of the masses. The pernicious description of an early visitor to Nashville, who had written that the local inhabitants were not panting for learning, was still applicable.

It was to private initiative that early education was indebted. Those who could afford it sent their children to one of the many private schools in the Nashville area.[4] In 1785, only five years after the settlement of Nashville, Davidson Academy had been chartered, and in 1817 the Nashville Female Academy was opened. Both institutions were exerting wide influence at the mid-century. The establishment of the first public school system in the South coupled with the firmly established private schools and colleges were significant factors in earning for Nashville her future apellation "Athens of the South."

Nashvillians, in the decade of the 1850's, set about to seek the education and enlightenment that could bring to them a richer, fuller and a more satisfying life. The story of their quest for knowledge and culture was boldly written in the accomplishments of a free school system, the contributions of private colleges and academies, the growth of libraries, and the erection of theaters and concert halls. The small Jewish community, finan-

95

cially incapable of guiding or promoting these undertakings, joined with the rest of the community as shareholders in a partnership for a better Nashville. This is the story of that search.

The unpopularity of free schools in Tennessee led to insufficient financial aid from the state.[5] Such feeble support could not attract the best teachers, resulting in the common or free school being designated as pauper schools.[6] Many parents, who could not afford private schools, preferred to keep their children at home rather than bear the stigma of attending a pauper school.[7]

On the local scene several factors prepared the way for a favorable acceptance of the free school. The first of these was the enactment of legislation that provided financial support. A tax of one-fifth of one per cent on city assessed property and a poll tax of two dollars on all white males, between the ages of twenty-one and fifty, were earmarked for public schools.[8] The second factor was the appointment of the eminent teacher, Alfred Hume, to investigate the public school systems of Philadelphia, New York and Boston. The advantages of public over private schools were stressed in Professor Hume's report to the city in August 1852. Plans were immediately set in motion that culminated in the erection of Nashville's first public school.[9]

Nashville Jewry of the early 1850's was predominantly an unmarried or a recently married group. Within its ranks there were few children of school age. These included Edwin, Caroline and Hans Hanf, native Tennesseans, Morris and Bernard Powers, Martin Charles and Mary Sulzbacher, native Ohioans, and Matilda Harris, a native of Missouri.[10] It is entirely possible that these young people were among the 1123 children to whom tickets of admission had been issued.[11] Finally, after many delays, on February 26, 1855, the new school on the corner of Spruce and Broad Streets had its opening.

Hume School, named in honor of Alfred Hume, was a three story structure with twelve rooms. It had been erected to house the primary, intermediate, grammar and high school departments for both boys and girls; but the usual nearsightedness, characteristic of school planning, necessitated an immediate enlargement of quarters. To accommodate the enrollment, an adjoining building was immediately purchased for the Girl's High School, and during the first year nineteen rooms in various sections of the city were secured.[12] Making the schools free did not bring in all the children, but the free school experiment in Nashville was off to a good start.

The incorporation of South Nashville into the city in July 1855 added a second school to the city system. Trimble, the South Nashville school, had been built in 1852. By 1860 three more schools had been added, Hynes in 1857, Lincoln Hall in 1859 and in 1860 Howard, sometimes referred to in contemporary writings as College Hall. During these years the renting of additional rooms never ceased.[13]

Nashville was growing, and its Jewish community was attracting newcomers. There is every reason to believe that the recently arrived Lewis children, Mary, Aaron and Fannie, the four little Blums, Pauline, Joseph, Jane and Louise, and Meyer and Solomon Cohen[14] were a small segment of this growing school census.

Public schools of the 1850's did not offer any education to the free blacks of the city. As early as March 1833 a small school for free Negro children had opened to which also came a few slaves through the permission of their white owners. Because of illness this school soon closed, but in 1838 a second school was started by white teachers. There followed a series of openings and closings until 1858 when the school had its final closing.[15]

The elementary school was divided into primary, intermediate and grammar departments. Each division stressed the 3 R's, reading, 'riting and 'rithmetic. With the required equipment of large black slate and slate pencils, the fashionable and flowery handwriting could be practiced over and over and over again. School rooms had little to offer in maps and blackboards, but the boys and girls learned of the world and history via the school readers. The selections in the readers emphasized the moral values to be found in thrift, honesty and charity.[16] Declamation and singing shared honors in popularity. Every boy had visions of being a second Daniel Webster as he conscientiously practiced the gestures and inflections that the current oratory demanded.

Orthoepy was the rage. A master of this art of phonetics was Mr. William Mulkey. After forty years of teaching languages, Mr. Mulkey authored a spelling book. His ability in training the voice to make the forty-one elemental sounds for which there was no rule of spelling was demonstrated in his public school and private classes.[17] An advertising gimmick employed by Mr. Mulkey in February 1857 was a public demonstration of a small German lad in the intricacies of producing the same sounds from various spellings.[18] Perhaps young Leopold Sobel from Austria or Prussian born Harris Heims was the assistant. If not, they learned Mulkey's rule that "the long sound of A preceding the dental sound of D" produced five different spellings such as fade, played, paid, obeyed and weighed.[19]

The popular Friday afternoon spelling bee had its premiere at Hynes School in February 1857 during a special reading and spelling exhibition. This display of pupil talent was so well received that plans were immediately inaugurated for weekly sessions to be held at the several schools.[20]

The pupil was generally taught what not to say rather than what to say in the dreary grammar class.[21] The errors that plagued the Southern child, the use of taint for is not, haint for have not and waunt for was not, presented a lesser problem for the Jewish child who in the great majority of cases was a first generation American privileged to learn a new language from the school room rather than an unlearned parent. Troublesome grammar difficulties for the Jewish child stemmed from verb usage and verb order. Young Anna and Isaac Levy, natives of Poland, undoubtedly, substituted the vocal sound of the consonant v for w and the difficult th invariably came forth as z.

"Spare the rod and spoil the child" was the golden rule in child guidance. The public school was strict and often harsh. The Board of Education published a book of rules and often each teacher made her own. There was to be no loitering to and from school.[22] Many suspensions followed infractions of rules.[23] In a five hour school day with only fifteen minutes allowed for recess, it was well nigh impossible for the school child to refrain from talking or smiling to a friend. For such forbidden behavior a punishment of smarting strokes on the palm of the culprit's hand was promptly administered.[24]

The education of the foreign Jew arriving in Nashville in this decade compared very favorably with the native of Nashville. Julius Ochs, Bertha Levy and Gustavus Schiff had attended European universities and spoke several languages. Henry Harris, Isaac Garritson, Alexander Iser and Jonas Heilbon were well grounded in Hebrew and Jewish literature. Many, however, had no formal education and probably could neither read nor write in their native language. The Jewish boy had one advantage over the boys of other faiths both native and foreign, as an adherence to Jewish tradition demanded that he be instructed until the age of thirteen when in a *Bar Mitsvoh* ceremony he would assume his obligation as a Jew. This custom was being observed here locally judging from the succession of advertisements in Jewish periodicals seeking not only a Rabbi but a qualified teacher.

The importance placed on the education of the boy did not always extend to the girl. Both her secular and formal religious education were often neglected. This failure in American life was observed and deprecated by the traveler, I. J. Benjamin.[25]

An adherence to Goethe's "Early let woman learn to serve for that is her calling," characterized the education of the female until far into the twentieth century. The popular belief that schooling for girls would tax the strength of the weaker sex limited her to a curriculum of art, needle work, china painting and music. The Nashville private female seminaries were well prepared for such a program and were particularly ably staffed in both vocal and instrumental music. In 1857 there were 563 day or ornamental students in the Nashville Female Academy.[26] This large enrollment indicated a desire on the part of local citizens to educate their daughters in the realm of beauty and refinement.

For practical reasons many girls received vocational training.

Mrs. M. E. Thompson's Sewing School on Union Street appealed to girls who desired to become seamstresses. This school boasted a special time saving system for both cutting and fitting garments.[27]

Unsuccessful efforts had been made in the State Legislative Assembly of 1855-56 to create a teacher training school.[28] By 1860 the twelve State Normals in the country were to be found in nine of our Northern states.[29] On the local level fourteen teachers had formed in 1848 the Tennessee High School for the education of school teachers.[30] The new Hume High School offered courses in teacher training. Six former Hume pupils were employed in the 1860 school system.[31]

Music lessons were a must. Parents saved and stinted to accumulate for the weekly or semi-weekly lessons. An accomplished youthful pianist of this decade was Morris Powers who astonished everyone in a recital in 1859 with his masterly playing of Gottschalk's "Bamboula" and "Home Sweet Home" with variations.[32]

Private instructions in music, undoubtedly, suffered in competition with the very successful Nashville Academy of Music and Fine Arts which was opened in 1855 by two German music professors Henry Weber and Charles Hess. Music attracted all ages and both sexes as did the waltzes, polkas and mazurkas taught in the several dancing schools. To learn the quadrille, as danced in Europe, one attended Mr. Goodwin's dancing class at the Odd Fellows Hall.[33] An appeal to the fairer sex was evidenced in Mr. Goodwin's special ladies classes. Here were taught "dances so gentle that the most delicate could practice them with safety."[34] Madame Julia Vincent's classes at the Harmonia Hall offered an even greater variety of instruction and included in addition to the popular lancers and quadrilles, the Spanish dance, the Highland Fling, the Horn Pipe and the Shawl dance.[35] Dancing was not an acceptable diversion to many church and lay people, but it found favor and approval from followers of the Jewish faith.

In the 1850's the city's most publicized institution for higher education was the University of Nashville, which had been established in 1785 as Davidson Academy. At no time during this decade were any Jewish students among its large enrollment in either its literary, law or medical departments. The literary college, having met with financial difficulties, merged in 1855 with the Western Military College of Princeton, Kentucky. The medical department ranked second in the country and by 1860 had graduated 768 doctors. In its nine year existence it had enrolled 2800 medical students.[36] The law school was created in 1854. A second medical school, Shelby Medical College, opened November 1, 1858; its connecting hospital for indigent sick was a worthy contribution in the realm of science and healing.

With few exceptions Nashville's young Jewish men were of foreign birth. They had risked the insecurity and loneliness of a new land to seek a new way of life and the paramount issue was one of sustenance. The $105 tuition charge for a term of twenty weeks[37] would have been difficult to come by and there were those left in the old homeland who needed every saved penny. No scholarships or loan funds were available for David Elsback, Jacob Bloomstein or Henry Schlessinger. We may conclude that Nashville's Jewish community was both too recent and too impoverished to have attained college status. The next two decades were to write a different version.

J. Emanuel was listed as a bookkeeper in the business directory for 1860. He very likely attended one of Nashville's three commercial colleges where bookkeeping, commercial law, commercial arithmetic and the indispensable penmanship were taught.[38] Calligraphy, a beautiful and legible handwriting, was considered a prime requisite for job seekers. The customary business letter of this era concluded with the phrase, "I remain your obedient servant;" and it would be written in practice books many times before the writer was rewarded with an elegant penmanship.

Adult education is not as recent a development in American life as is commonly thought. Subscription libraries, singing groups, dramatic clubs and an insatiable desire for the lecture platform characterized this era. These activities enriched the lives of the participants and gave evidence of their desire for knowledge. As early as 1842 the Mechanics Library Association had sponsored lectures on various subjects.[39] Horizons could be broadened very cheaply with the purchase of a family ticket at one dollar or a single admission for 12½ cents. During this decade people were eager to inform themselves and were willing to pay a travelling lecturer fifty to three hundred dollars a lecture.[40] Because it was a fruitful source of income many speakers and, undoubtedly, some charlatans were drawn to the lecture platform where they agreed to speak on every conceivable subject. *The New York Tribune* announced that 194 gentlemen and eight ladies, qualified lecturers for the 1859 season, would probably earn three to eight thousand dollars.[41]

In Nashville, lectures were sponsored by many groups. The Medical colleges, the Medical Association, the Tennessee Historical Society and churches sponsored speakers. In many instances lecturers sponsored themselves. They traveled from town to town advertising their appearance in the local papers.

The Rev. Orville Dewey, a giant in the lecture field, delivered his famous Lowell lectures in Nashville in January 1854. In a series of twelve lectures for three dollars Rev. Dewey attempted to impress his audience with their importance in a creative world. His subject was "The Problems of Human Destiny."[42] It is doubtful that the Nashville audience was as enthusiastic as the cultured Boston groups to which Rev. Dewey was accustomed. For sweet charity's sake Nashvillians listened to a lecture on "The Railway System of the United States."[43] For the pure love of science and only twenty-five cents, one heard Professor Hale's lecture at the Third Presbyterian Church on "Electro-Biology."[44] In a lighter vein Professor Copeland, a master in the realm of elocution, gave a demonstration of his histrionic talent in the Federal Court Room at the Capitol.[45]

The most fascinating lectures were those that accompanied the gigantic panoramas. This 1850 edition of Cinemascope offered as much excitement and beauty as the modern screen. The sound came from the lecturer explaining the breath-taking snows of the Arctic, the steep ascents on Mt. Blanc, the wondrous stalactites at Mammoth Cave. The audience breathlessly visited the gold fields of California, Westminster Abbey, Niagara Falls and many far away places.[46] It was a wonderful experience for these little traveled and semi-provincial people.

A petition that may have involved some of the Nashville Jewry was presented to the Board of Education in September 1859. The use of a room at Hynes School was requested by seventy-seven persons for the purpose of having taught at their expense a class in the German language. The Board did not grant permission, but it promised to make every effort to furnish a room in which both English and German would be taught.[47]

"The people of the South are not a bookish people."[48] This contemporary observation stemmed from the fact that of $16,000,000 worth of books published in 1856 the southern states could lay claim to only $750,000.[49] This accusation could not have been directed at Nashville because the local publishing houses, the largest being the Southern Methodist, claimed an annual business of $224,038 in 1858.[50]

The country was reading more than it ever had. An improvement in the invention of electrotyping had stimulated printing and lowered the costs so that the output of books increased 50% in the first half of the decade.[51] The local library associations, private libraries, book stores and newspapers gave evidence that the folks in Nashville were becoming inveterate readers.

There were no public libraries in either Nashville or Davidson County in 1850. The Mechanics Association had established a library in 1844, and by 1860 it had a collection of some 5,000 books, many of which were technical.[52] The library and reading rooms on College Street were open daily from 8 AM to 10 PM, and admission was free. However, an annual membership fee of three dollars entitled one to borrow books, attend monthly lectures and classes in drawing and engraving.[53] The Y.M.C.A. had a smaller circulating library of some 400 good standard works. Their reading room was well supplied with current newspapers and periodicals.[54] The 14,000 volume library of medical and academic books at the University of Nashville was the largest in the city. In addition it housed the collection of the college literary societies.[55] The most pretentious library was in the State Capitol. During the '50's, through appropriation of special funds and taxes, $12,000 had been spent on a library of 11,000 volumes and 4,000 pamphlets.[56] The Tennessee Historical Society owned about 900 books and possibly 1000 pamphlets by 1860.[57] In addition to adequate church libraries there existed many private libraries of considerable worth and size.[58]

The favorite meeting place for book lovers was Berry's Bookstore. It stocked one of the finest collections of contemporary literature that was to be found anywhere in the country.[59] Furnished with cushioned chairs for the convenience of customers, it gave the appearance of a literary club.[60]

In this golden era of American literature were the people reading the works of Poe, Emerson, Longfellow or Whittier? The advertisements of the three local bookstores, Berry's, Hagan's, Smith and York's indicated a preference for English authors, especially Dickens and Scott.

The most important book of the century, Charles Darwin's *Origin of the Species* published in 1857, was far outranked in readers by the best sellers, *Ten Nights in a Bar Room* and *Uncle Tom's Cabin.* There was a definite preference for the master storyteller, Mrs. E.D.E.N. Southworth, an artist in the creation of melodramatic and thrilling plots involving sweet innocent heroines and despicable villains. Teen-age girls, mothers and grandmothers lived vicariously in Mary J. Holme's tragedies and romances, the most popular being *Lena Rivers* and *Tempest and Sunshine.* The first dime novel *Malaeska* by Ann Sophia Stevens appeared in 1860 and placed women novelists in the ranks of best sellers. Marriage counselling found its way into print in an eight volume series called *Clarissa or the History of a Young Lady.* The author, Samuel Richardson, discussed the important "concerns of private life, particularly the misconduct of parents in relation to marriage."[61] As the war years drew near the Southern press fought a vigorous campaign against Northern literature.

The Jewish home usually contained a few books on ceremonial and holiday observances; many of these were cherished family heirlooms brought from the old country.[62] The destruction by fire in 1850 of the first American Jewish Publication Society had deprived Jewry of any sponsoring agency for the publication of Jewish and religious literature. Communities looked to Rabbi Isaac Leeser of Philadelphia for guidance in the selection and purchasing of books for home and synagogue use. The Nashville Jewish community in its celebrated "five family, eight young men" letter of 1852 made a request of Rabbi Leeser for the purchase of an English translated prayer book and the Five Books of Moses.

The newspapers, the influential institution in American life, always astonished foreign visitors by their numbers and the importance attached to them. Three of the four pages of the poorly printed five local dailies of 1860 were devoted to advertisements much of which was quackery. Intolerant editorials, meager local information, national and international news were condensed into the space of one page. Only Nashvillians of high position were deemed newsworthy.

Foreign news came with ships until after the event of August 16, 1858, when Queen Victoria and President Buchanan exchanged greetings by telegraph. Foreign news items were captioned "Latest from Europe" or "Foreign Intelligence." Nashvillians of this era read about the bravery of the Australians, discontent in India, Peary in Japan, the birth of octuplets in Ohio[63] but little about local happenings. Undoubtedly, Nashville news was being adequately publicized by word of mouth. Eagerly awaited were the *Gazette's* listing of uncalled for letters at the postoffice, daily river news with schedules of boat arrivals and departures, train and coach schedules.

The sensational murder trial of the decade concerned the killing of Philip Key, son of Francis Scott Key, by the socially prominent member of Congress, Daniel Sickles. It had all the earmarks of a modern whodunit and was avidly read by both sexes.

The mounting crusades for women's rights[64] caught the attention of many local women readers, who undoubtedly followed with interest the activities of the reforming Amelia Bloomer. *The Southern Ladies Companion* and the two locally published magazines *The Parlor Visitor* and *The Ladies Pearl* published receipts for cooking and needlework and fashion articles highlighting the Paris styles of Mme Pompadour. Their sentimental stories were concerned more with morality than with good literature requirements.

Harper's Weekly, Atlantic Monthly, DeBow's Review, Godey's Ladies' Book, Putnam's Monthly were a few of the most popular national journals sold in all the local bookstores and reviewed in the local newspapers. *Frank Leslie's Illustrated Newspaper,* a forerunner of modern illustrated journalism, appeared in 1855.

With the exception of the monthly *Occident and American Jewish Advocate,* all national Jewish periodicals were printed each Friday; and a subscription to each cost three dollars annually. Local congregational news, national problems and international Jewry were adequately discussed and kept the readers well-informed on current issues. The Jews of Denmark were discussed for six months in the columns of *The Asmonean.* Articles on the Jews of Copenhagen, Russia, Gibraltar, Calcutta, Sahara and China informed American Jewry of their brethren elsewhere in the world. For only twenty-five cents, notices of births, marriages and death would be publicized. The local Nashville dailies often printed excerpts from Jewish periodicals, particularly from *The Israelite* and *London Jewish Chronicle.*

The Republican Banner announced in 1861 that a German paper *Der Boebacher* would be published semi-weekly in Nashville.[65] The presence of a sufficiently large community of German citizenry was indicated by the need for such a paper. Until the 1870's the advertisements of the local Jewish congregation for a rabbi consistently required of applicants an ability to speak in both the English and German languages.

An important factor in the establishment of the New Adelphi Theater in 1850[66] was the realization that the theater was a potential cultural influence. Theater was not new to Nashville one having opened on December 4, 1807. During the 1850's the Adelphi was also called Nashville Theater, and later it was renamed the Gaiety. For religious reasons many Nashvillians refused to attend concerts at a theater; so many performances were presented at either Douglas Hall, the Odd Fellows Hall, or the Masonic Hall.

The greatest sensation of the decade was Jenny Lind, the Swedish soprano. Brought to America by the showman P. T. Barnum, she earned in her two year American tour over $130,000. In the spring of 1851 Jenny sang at the newly built Adelphi which had to be enlarged for her concerts. Tickets sold for as high as $200, and standing room brought three dollars.[67] The audience, so entranced with her rendition of Home Sweet Home, forgot the uncomfortable rough plank seats and drafty hall.[68] In honor of the wonderful Jenny, bonnets, jewelry, shawls, gloves, flour and meats were named. In Nashville one could buy Jenny Lind hats and Jenny Lind billiard tables.[69] Ben Lyons, local Jewish business man, named his refreshment hall, the Jenny Lind saloon.

Although scenes from grand opera had been presented in Nashville many times, the first entire opera was given on May 24, 1854.[70] It is doubtful that the Nashville audience, which had proved itself liberal patrons of minstrelsy, was either familiar with opera technique or had acquired the taste and discernment for a real appreciation of the Italian company of forty artists which played here for five nights.[71]

Minstrelsy was a passion and the fashion in the 1850's. A fondness for jigs and reels and the folksy melodies of Stephen Foster found an appreciation and responsive audience among Nashvillians. The favorites among the Negro character delineators were Joe Sweeney's Virginia Minstrels and Campbell's Minstrels.

Among the Swiss Bell Ringers who had been delighting Nashville audiences since 1846[72] was the skillful Peake family who always appeared in native costume. Ventriloquists, magicians, Chinese jugglers and variety shows included Nashville in their Hinterland circuit. On April 10, 1854 the French ballet delighted a local audience most of whom were completely unacquainted with this art form.[73]

Excitement was in the air on an April day in 1854. Down near the Cumberland River a crowd of men, women and children had gathered to see Van Amburgh's circus of lions, elephants and hippos which had just arrived on a large floating palace.[74] This was the heydey of the circus. As early as 1800 it had attained such popularity that thirty different shows were touring the country. The circus audience had one major difference with that of other forms of entertainment; it attracted a larger element of children. The comedy of the monkeys and the horsemanship of the equestriennes thrilled the young folks. In all likelihood, among the laughing boys and girls enjoying the antics of the dean of American clowns, Dan Rice, there might have been the youthful Levick sisters Rachel and Eva, or the Levy brothers Sol and Raphael. Very definitely they were on hand to view the free street parades that preceded the performance, for the sight of forty horses, four abreast, marching down College Street, was for young and old, sheer enjoyment.

"The play's the thing." So said Mr. Shakespeare and so echoed Nashville audiences. The stock companies of the 1850's produced a constant stream of dramas, farces and comedies. Theater goers were fascinated by the heavy villains; they wept for betrayed, sweet innocence. Eliza Logan, Charlotte Cushman and Julia Dean received accolades of most popular, most capable and most beautiful. The Hamlet and Richard III of the Shakespearean stars, James Murdoch and Edwin Booth, filled the playhouse and brought forth raves from the press. Booth attracted the largest audience since the appearance of the great Jenny Lind.[75] Other favorites included the comedian Joe Cowell and the Irish delineator, John Drew.

The few Jewish play-goers were probably warm supporters of their co-religionist, Adah Menken. Although Mrs. Menken had great personal charm, she was not a forceful or even a good actress. In light comedy she was adequate and often clever. During one of her visits to Nashville, Mrs. Menken convinced the manager that Lady Macbeth was one of her triumphs. The night the curtain rolled up on that play, she had not familiarized herself with the role and had to be fed the lines by the star, James Murdoch. Undoubtedly, Mrs. Menken succeeded in giving the Nashville audience the most remarkable performance of Lady Macbeth that it had been their misfortune to witness.

Willingly the lady returned to more familiar roles, and everyone was happier.[76]

At the conclusion of a tour, a benefit would customarily be tendered the star or the manager. The names of Benjamin and Jacob Lyons, fervent supporters of the legitimate theater, appeared several times during the decade among the names of such donors.[77]

The local press repeatedly reprimanded theater goers for their behavior. They accused them of possessing no critical judgement and of invariably applauding at the wrong time. If they liked anything they shrieked. Mrs. Sam Cowell, wife of the famous English variety actor, described the area as a "region of roarers."[78] Little regard for spectators was shown in the late arrival of the ladies and the early departure of the men. As soon as the outcome of the play was apparent many would "run out as though the house was on fire." The refreshment room and the drinking saloon only added further confusion, as the men went up and down to drink, to buy plug tobacco and to engage in fist fights.[79]

To many and particularly to the local German group, amateur theatricals and musicales brought the greatest pleasure. The Nashville Dramatic Club, a group of "respectable and intelligent young men," had gained favorable comment in their first appearance.[80] The productions of the German Harmonia Club, a social and dramatic group, were often given in the German language and drew large audiences to productions that merited the accolade of professional. In 1857 the group rented and fitted up its own Harmonia Hall, where, following the dramatic presentations, the seats would be removed for an evening of dancing.[81] A third Little Theatre group, the Robertson Dramatic Club, was an affiliate of the Robertson Association, a local charitable organization interested in care of the sick and destitute.[82] Jacob Lyons, secretary of the Robertson Dramatic Club, merited favorable comment for his performance as a bailiff in March 1857.[83] The Hook and Ladder company, the Protestant Orphanage and the House of Industry were a few of the beneficiaries of the many productions for charity sponsored by the local dramatic groups.[84]

Undoubtedly, Nashville was indebted to the German element for the encouragement they gave the musical world. They sponsored the musical event of the decade, the Schiller Music Festival in celebration of the 100th anniversary of the great German poet.[85] They were also instrumental in the presentation of Hayden's Oratorio, *The Creation*, in 1858 and Handel's *Messiah* in 1859.[86]

Every parent makes a sympathetic and appreciative audience for its own child's performance. The many concerts, dramatic presentations and declamations may not have broadened the mama's and papa's horizons as much as they swelled their chests with pride, but they served as wonderful experiences in home and school cooperation.

As 1860 drew to a close and the war clouds grew darker, Nashvillians could look back on the wonderful decade of the 1850's as a time of seeking wider vistas through enlightenment.

CHAPTER VII

A Time to Laugh

The chronicle of American life and manners was woven by a traditional gospel of work. The commonplace lives of the vast majority of Nashville's citizens and certainly most of its Jewry were circumscribed by long arduous days uncurbed by state or federal legislation.[1] Few hours remained for relaxation or amusement. A time to laugh, a time for diversion, a time set apart from the workaday world were to be found in the observance of national and religious holidays, in church and synagogue affiliation and in the everyday contacts with friends, neighbors and relatives.

Immigrants learned quickly the preference for Independence Day as the number one national holiday. Each year the country's fight for "life, liberty and the pursuit of happiness" was retold in flaming oratory embellished by parading men amidst the firing of cannons, the shooting of firecrackers and the eating of popcorn. The Germans fell victims of the marching fever. Their target shooting group known as the German Yaegers donned their colorful red-corded gray and green uniforms for the July 4th celebrations. They won both envy and admiration for their precision marching and turning.[2] Barbecues, picnics and fish frys were features of the day's activities. An occasional steam-boat excursion[3] or balloon ascension[4] added excitement and varied the program. A dance or cotillion inevitably concluded this memorable day.

The annual state fair, inaugurated in 1857,[5] provided a week of pleasure for citizens of Davidson and surrounding counties. The exhibits of handwork, art, preserving and canning captured the women's interest. Men were attracted to the farm products, live stock, manufactured articles and marble work. But the

111

events of the turf, the trotters and horses drawn tandem, created thrills and excitement for all.

Oftimes the week of the Fair coincided with the two most important holidays in the Jewish calendar. Although a discussion of these holy days pertains to the chapter "A Time To Build Up," one must be mindful that holidays, regardless of their holy and spiritual intent, were eagerly awaited by Jewry as a time of pleasure and relaxation. The first of the Fall holidays was the New Year or *Rosh Ha Shonah*. This ushered in a ten day period of penitence ending in the fast on the Day of Atonement or *Yom Kippur*. Five days after these awesome and holy Fall holidays, the Jews observed the *Succos* or Festival of the Harvest. This festival dates back to the time of the exodus when Jews fleeing in the wilderness were forced to live in temporary booths. It has been annually observed by Jews as a time of thanksgiving and prayer. Children particularly delighted in partaking of meals for one week in unroofed booths. These temporary shelters were erected in the back yards by the men of the family; the decorations of fruit, vegetables and branches were arranged by the young people.

Hence it is understandable that the phenomenon of a thanksgiving day was no new experience for Jewry. The American Thanksgiving afforded the family an opportunity for family visiting and feasting.

Almost simultaneously with the Christian holiday, Christmas, the Jew observed the Feast of Lights, *Chanukah*. This festival commemorated a victory over oppression in the days of the Syrian ruler Antiochus IV. It was primarily a home celebration lasting for eight nights. Candles were lit, one for the first night, two for the second until the eighth night when eight candles were lit. Along with the exchange of gifts, prayers were said, and songs were sung. Christmas was not unknown to the Jewish immigrant. The retelling and reenacting of the Nativity story had been occasions for much discrimination and persecution. Perhaps a desire to erase differences contributed to the acceptance in many Jewish homes of the custom of hanging children's stockings for St. Nick's visit. No Jew would ever have acknowledged that such an action was tantamount to observing a holiday completely foreign and antagonistic to his own beliefs.

Sh'lach monas, the giving of gifts or generosity to the poor, was identified with *Purim,* the Feast of Lots. On the eve of *Purim* the Jewish community in masquerade costumes repaired to the small rented synagogue on North Market Street for an evening of mirth and merrymaking. To the traditional reading of the *Megillah,* Book of Esther, upon which the festival is based, the children unrestrainedly added the accompaniment of noisemakers, the signal being the reader's mention of the name of the arch anti-semite Haman. A play or a dance would conclude this happy and memorable day.

On the heels of the Purim celebration, Ireland's national holiday St. Patrick's day was commemorated by the Irish element with the wearing of the green and much conviviality.

The two spring holidays, the Christian Easter and the Jewish Passover or *Pesach,* were observed simultaneously. During the week of Passover the Jews ate unleavened bread or *matzos* in remembrance of the exodus from Egyptian bondage. On the eve of the holiday the family would gather from near and far for the festive home or *Seder* service. The Jacob Hyman family, undoubtedly, had difficulty finding places for all the family that came to celebrate. Mrs. Hyman was a sister of B. M. Myers and mother of Mrs. Sam Powers, Mrs. Mike Powers and Mrs. Myer Joseph, all residents of Nashville. During grandfather Jacob Hyman's reading from the *Hagadah* of the flight to freedom, little Louis Powers was permitted to ask the age old question, "Why is this night different from all other nights?" All joined in the songs and games which followed a traditional Passover meal.

The festival of *Shevuos* was observed seven weeks after Passover. This holiday commemorated the giving of the Torah to Moses on Mt. Sinai.

All Jews looked forward to the Sabbath. The joys and pleasures of the day more than compensated for its restrictions. In addition to a day of rest it served through synagogue and home service to strengthen family ties. No matter how poorly one lived all week, for the Sabbath every effort was made to provide food for both the stomach and the mind. Special delicacies came to be associated with the day. Sabbath afternoons were devoted to visiting and study. The learned men of the Jewish community probably gathered at the home of either Henry Harris or Alexander Iser for discussions of Biblical or Talmudic law.

The only permissible Sunday activities for the Christian were church attendance and visiting.[6] In the 1850's folks amused themselves by just talking. Since the Jew observed Saturday as his Sabbath both he and his German Christian friends were criticized for their unrestricted Sunday activities. Germans loved beer and were not averse to beer gardens, card playing or chess games as Sunday diversions. The church frowned on cards, games of chance and dancing on any day of the week.

As friends visited back and forth, they exhibited their shell, button and autograph collections. A favorite entertainment was seeing the world via the stereoscope. The distinctly American custom of the surprise party, planned minutely weeks in advance, was popular in this decade. It surprised only the honored guest who had just settled down for a quiet evening to suddenly become the victim of invading and oftimes unwanted guests. The familiar expression "stuck on a girl" was created at taffy pulls. It was popular with the unmarried group; it gave the young man an excuse for putting his arms around his girl as he helped in the job of candy pulling.

The foreign element enjoyed dancing. Lusky's Hall on Broad Street was the scene of many balls[7] and the German Harmonia Club invariably concluded their concerts and dramatic presentations with a dance.

The summer season offered much in the way of recreation. Picnic's at Magnolia Gardens on Mrs. White's turnpike, outings at Watkin's Grove, walks to Sulphur Springs, swimming and fishing at Stone's river, ice cream suppers, the new soda fount, croquet, tennis, target shooting and pitching horse shoes provided Nashvillians with many happy hours.

Visiting celebrities and notables created excitement. The visit of ex-president Millard Fillmore on May 4, 1854, was long remembered and discussed.

All religions regard the marriage rites as sacred. In the Jewish home, the social which inevitably followed the religious vows was a gay and often noisy affair. Three "elegant" weddings of this decade meriting newspaper notices were the double wedding of Samuel Lyons to Miss Elizabeth Isaaks of Bristol, England and Jacob Lyons to Miss Louisa Delisser of Chattanooga[8] and the marriage of Julius Ochs to Miss Bertha Levy of Nashville. The Reverend Alexander Iser officiated at both ceremonies. The Ochs-Levy nuptials were accompanied by "three bottles of sparkling catawba."[9]

The annual election of synagogue officers provided a training ground for aspiring leaders. At these spirited meetings tempers flared, and sensibilities were wounded. It is likely that the 1859 split in the congregation grew out of such a meeting.

During the 1850's the gospel of work which had characterized American life had broadened to a creed of "work and acquire." Man's increasing preoccupation with the business of making money resulted in the establishment of wealth as the yardstick for a new and growing aristocracy. The palatial homes and new public buildings, the mushrooming public resorts and commercial amusements gave evidence that in this decade Nashville possessed a sizeable, wealthy and pleasure seeking social group.[10] The 1860 census revealed that three Jews, Sinai Nathan, Michael Powers and Isaac Stein had amassed fortunes of over $10,000.

For seven dollars a week or $1.25 a day, one could enjoy not only excellent food and good music but "invigorating air, cooling shade and curative waters" at the near-by Tyree, Epperson, Beer-Sheba, Red-Boiling and Hurricane Springs. The half-price rates for children and servants were slightly below those extended the family horse.[11] At near-by farms the same invigorating air and good food were available for those who could not afford the luxury of a summer resort. Lookout Mountain, a picturesque resort near Chattanooga, was unsurpassed in scenic beauty. Few Nashvillians visited the fashionable Saratoga Springs where the object was to see and be seen. However, they were informed through the local newspapers of the "battle of the dress," an annual contest at this New York State resort. As ladies vied for attention and prominence, they paraded a succession of stylish outfits. During the summer of 1857 it was not until the appearance of the sixty-third dress that one lady won out in this war of fashion.[12]

Throughout the country commercial amusements sprouted. The first gate receipts in 1858 from baseball embarked that recently created game in the field of spectator sports.[13] On the local scene, billiards were enjoying great popularity. Ben and Lewis Lyons were responsible for stimulating interest in the game through local exhibitions of world renowned experts.[14] Ben appealed to feminine players by establishing a special ladies' billiard parlor. Very likely, local Jewry viewed with more consternation than interest the presence of a co-religionist, Barney Aaron, in the prize fighting ring.[15] The heavy-weight champion John Heenan elicited interest because of his marriage to the Jewish darling of the stage Adah Menken.

The popular horse race, rooted in the early settlers' love for stockbreeding and horsemanship, had been legalized in the state to develop native stock. To the newly arrived immigrant a horse was a business investment. Ownership of one denoted an advance up the economic ladder, from pack peddler by foot to peddler via horse and wagon. But for the fashionable Nashville set, the spring and fall races at the Nashville course were highlights in this exciting sport of kings. To accommodate the crowds, new audience stands and new buildings were erected in 1860.[16]

The gambler was also attracted to the races. The gambling passion was inherent in the American nature. Believing in the principle "nothing ventured, nothing gained," men gambled on anything from horse racing and cock fighting to guessing the number of peas in a pod.

The greatest opportunities for speculation were to be found in the popular lotteries. In early America, lotteries had been a respectable means of raising money for defense, canals, hospitals, churches and schools. It was as respectable to sell lottery tickets as to sell Bibles.[17] About the middle of the 1830's most states, Tennessee included, legislated against lotteries. Suffering and bankruptcy had followed the spending of food and rent money on such tickets of chance. The idea grew that lotteries were morally wrong. However, most folks had no objections to winning large fortunes with one lucky stroke. They continued to invest thousands in the Havana, Grand Duchy of Baden, Georgia, Baltimore and Alabama lotteries. This racket took out of Nashville $100,000 in one year. Of this, $75,000 went into the Havana lottery which offered a better investment, as fewer tickets were sold. The local *Daily Gazette* campaigned for the removal of restrictions against lotteries claiming that money could be kept at home and channeled into local projects.[18] However, folks kept building castles in the air, as one lucky ticket promised wealth and security.

America had been described by the French visitor De Tocqueville as "a nation of joiners." During the 1850's, first generation Jewish Americans sought membership in groups that were almost 100% German. In such affiliations there existed a rapport that was not possible in the often closed ranks of the native society. The Independent Order of Odd Fellows established its first lodge in Nashville in 1839; by 1860 it had grown to four lodges and two encampments.[19] The Aurora Lodge 105, established in 1858, conducted its meetings in the German language.[20] A charter member of the group, Sinai Nathan, served as the first treasurer. Jacob Lyons was a scribe of Encampment no. 1, and his brother Ben served in the same capacity for Olive Branch encampment.[21]

In 1796 the Masonic order was established in Nashville. It received its charter from the Grand Lodge of North Carolina. Only two lodges existed during the 1850's, Cumberland no. 8 and Phoenix no. 131.[22] Since no membership records are now available, it is not known if any Jews were members of this order in the '50's. The Germania Lodge 355 was chartered in 1868, and records reveal that E. Wolf and Dr. Gustavus Schiff were officers of this branch.[23]

An editorial appeared in the local press in 1854 in defense of the German Turn Verein. Organized in Cincinnati in 1848 it was accused of being anti-constitutional and dangerous to the welfare of the country. The national president made known the aims of the open membership group as "an association to invigorate body, mind and improve health."[24] The Turn Verein was not chartered in Nashville until 1865.[25]

Men created opportunities for almost nightly excursions. Lodge and club meetings were scheduled weekly. Memberships in the Masons, the Odd Fellows, a chess club, a dramatic club and the volunteer fire brigade could successfully shorten the hours at home.

The volunteer "fire-eaters," expecting no reward, only smiles of approval, had existed for twenty-three years. Upon the creation of Nashville's first paid fire department in July 1860, the volunteers were honorably discharged.[26] Throughout the decade the group had heeded all fire alarms. In 1851 it became necessary to organize an auxiliary fire guard which had police powers while on duty. This police group of some sixty or seventy members kept the streets clear in the vicinity of the fire, prevented citizens from interfering with the active fireman and kept a good lookout for thieves or plunderers.[27] The bucket brigade gave way to the first fire engine in 1858, and the following year the first four wheel steam engine was purchased. By 1860 the fire department comprised five companies and a hook and ladder company. The six hundred members of the department were represented by an elected committee of nine in matters of interest to the department.[28] The decade was marked by many disastrous fires. In 1856 the Masonic Hall, the Davidson County Court House and many buildings on the Public Square were destroyed. The Courthouse was fired again in 1857, and in 1860 the famous St. Cloud hotel was destroyed by fire. Mayor Randal McGavock in his message to the city council in 1859 reported thirty-nine fires and seventy-four false alarms for the year.[29] The German population of the city at their own expense had equipped a hook and ladder company with hooks, poles, ladders and buckets.[30] Active members of the volunteer fire brigade included Ben Myers, Judah Frankland[31] and Ben Lyons.[32]

As postmen were not introduced until 1866 the post-office was a busy and popular site for the local citizenry. It maintained a daily service from 6:30 A.M. to 7:30 P.M. except Sunday when the office was opened from 7:30 A.M. to 9 A.M. and from 5 P.M. to 7 P.M.[33] In anticipation of a letter from the old country or from a recently arrived relative, the local Jewish settlers, undoubtedly, daily visited the post-office. Martin Sulzbacher looked for a message from his step brother Morris Cohn, who had left Nashville in 1853 to become one of earliest settlers in Leavenworth, Kansas.[34] The young bride Esther Lande hoped for a letter from her sisters, the Misses Boxim of New York City.[35] Until 1847 the postage system was a pay as you receive arrangement. Postage stamps were then introduced, and either the sender or the recipient could pay the postage. The rates were reduced in 1851 to three cents prepaid or five cents unpaid for one-half ounce carried three thousand miles.[36] In order to save money, travelers were besieged with requests to carry letters and packages to the city of destination. The Garritson letter, from which the title of this book was borrowed, was personally delivered to Rabbi Leeser of Philadelphia by Louis Hanf of Nashville. By 1854, mail from New York arrived in Nashville via coach and river in three and one-half days.[37] Schedules were often upset by frozen rivers. The names of persons for whom mail was held at the post-office were published in the *Nashville Daily Gazette*. This service, very likely, gained many subscribers.

The journey to market, to school, to church and to friends was accomplished via the shoe-leather express. For greater distances, families of wealth maintained horses and carriages or from livery stables, one could hire horses, buggies and even drivers. On holidays the demand far exceeded the supply. A member of the "Hebrew children," whose name was withheld, was arrested for fast driving and fined nine and one-half dollars in the spring of 1857.[38] By 1860, several private omnibus companies operated within the city and suburban areas. Trips were made hourly; fares were five cents; departing and arriving trains were met.[39]

"Nashville can boast the finest capitol in the Union."[40] The classic State building for which the cornerstone had been laid in 1845 achieved for the city an international prominence. Unanimous appraisal of its magnificence was evident in the comments to be found in contemporary gazateers, guide books and writings of American and foreign visitors.[41] From its imposing position atop the high Campbell's Hill, it commanded a view of the surrounding territory and was easily visible to all as they approached the city.

The decade of the fifties was characterized by a boom in public and private building. The "Bloody Row" on the South side of the Square, where once the whiskey shops had reared their ghastly fronts, had given way to a row of fine wholesale houses.[42] A remodelled City Hall, new theater, public schools, Masonic Hall, Odd Fellow Building, churches of various denomination and the new Maxwell House Hotel, for which the cornerstone was laid August 23, 1860, signified a flourishing and progressive city.

In 1860 four-fifths of the people of the United States lived in the country. Perhaps half of these lived in log cabins of one or two rooms.[43] Within Nashville many new residential areas with palatial homes were being developed. However, the majority of the people continued to live within walking distance of the downtown shopping area. No Jews resided in the fashionable residential district of the fifth ward which included Summer, High and Vine Streets between Broad and Cedar. The Aaron Landes, the David Elsbachs, the Alexander Isers and the H. H. Goldbergs lived in the recently incorporated South Nashville area. The home addresses for the majority of the Jewish families in 1860 were North Market and South Market Street. City planning was evident in the numbering of the houses which was completed in February 1853.[44]

The attached house sat close to the street on a small lot with yard and garden in the rear. It was being replaced by a more pretentious home which possessed a front veranda for rocking

120

and for watching passerbys. An occasional iron fence added a decorative note along with the front steps, foot-scraper and hitching post. For $2000 one could purchase a seven room house with a modern bay window. Despite the many handsome private residences, there existed unsightly dirty areas that cried out for slum clearance.[45]

A study of the 1860 census reveals that it was not uncommon for many families to occupy a one residence building. With Rabbi Jonas Heilbon and wife lived Mr. and Mrs. Nathan Rosenthar and two children. The Morris Luskys were joint tenants with Marks and Julia Adyson and four months old Anne. Eleven people occupied the residence of Michael Schwartz. Mr. and Mrs. Schwartz lodged their married daughters Rebecca Attelsohn and Rose Abrahams with their respective husbands and young babies, both named Hanna. The Sam Shyers and the Michael Shyers occupied the same dwelling on Broad Street. In all likelihood it also served as their business address. It was quite common for these early immigrants to occupy a few rooms behind or over their place of business. The home and business addresses were the same for J. Green on Broad Street and for Z. Levy also on Broad.

In the outlying regions the ability to sink a well at no great depth was the first consideration in the purchase of a lot. In these suburban areas, families owned horses, cows, and chickens. Jacob Bloomstein was the only Jew whose residence was given in the 1860 census outside the city limits.

Within the house a fashionable ugliness reigned. In a fast growing country there had been little time to think of furniture in terms of art. The recent invention of the jig-saw and carving machine brought to the middle classes quantities of massive furniture heavily marked with scrolls, curves and carvings. A death blow had been dealt the cabinet maker; simplicity had been sacrified for ostentation.

The parlor of the 1850's was off limits to the family except for Sabbath visiting, piano practicing, weddings and funerals. For this sad and solemn occasion, invitations were frequently sent. Biblical and Talmudic law made it mandatory that the

Jewish corpse be interred within a short period. Consequently notice got around to the Jewish community by word of mouth.[46]

Standard furnishings of the parlor included a marble top table with crystal oil lamp, a horsehair sofa, a rush bottom Windsor chair and wall to wall Brussel's carpeting. A Currier and Ives print of "God Bless Our Home" and family portraits adorned the papered walls. The increasing popularity of photographs over the more expensive oil painting was due to revolutionary improvements in picture making. However, having a likeness taken required standing in front of a camera immovable as a statue for at least a minute. For those who were unable to maintain a steady position, the head would be clamped between prongs so arranged as not to show in the picture.

What-nots bursting with bric-a-brac, chalk figurines and sea shells offered a variety of conversation pieces. The rumbling noise of the shells reminded young Simon and Henry Klein of the Atlantic Ocean waves they had so recently heard. A fondness for fringe and tassels was visible on curtains, tablecloths and the indispensable portieres which served to separate the parlor from the dining area.

The dining room in the homes of the wealthy displayed beautiful silver, Bohemian cut glass, French china and exquisite Irish linen damask. Isaac Stein was Nashville's wealthiest Jew.[47] In all likelihood, his young wife Rosalie possessed these elegant appointments.

The conventional bedroom contained a wardrobe or bureau, wash stand, table and bedstead. The latter was often so high that it required the use of steps to be reached. A popular style of this era was the bedstead of high posts covered with a canopy from which beautiful draperies hung.[48]

By 1860, many homes boasted hot and cold water and a modern innovation, the bathtub. As early as 1854 Currey Furniture Co. advertised the shower apparatus for bathing.[49] The first bathtub had been installed in the White House in 1850 during the regime of President Fillmore.

Housewives were interested in the new patents and improvements that lightened their duties. In the realm of kitchen gadgetry, the bainmarie or double boiler, the corn sheller, apple parer, non-failure fruit canning top, five minute ice-cream freezer, water cooler and fly trap served as time saving equipment.[50]

On the national scene refrigeration got a tremendous boost from the patent for ice manufacturing in 1860. However ice was not manufactured in Nashville until 1880.[51] It was cut in the winter from local ponds or rivers, stored in ice houses or imported in the summer from other areas where it had been stored. The Lake Kingston ice house near the wharf had a storage capacity of three thousand pounds.[52] Housewives bought ice from a delivery ice-cart. More and more housewives were purchasing the new self-ventilating refrigerator,[53] a great improvement over the old ice chest and spring house.

Knowledge of food preservation was a must. Salt used generously as a preservative for butter and meats was also used to pack eggs. It excluded air and prevented breakage.[54] Altho commercial canneries began to flourish in the 1850's, housewives continued to can fruits, vegetables, preserves and pickles. Only five million cans of food were bought by the thirty-five million population in 1856 averaging for each American in that year one-seventh of a can.[55]

Nashville housewives bought milk from men who delivered in large milk cans. Fresh fruits and vegetables, obtainable at the market house, were excluded from the diet of small children. As in most cities, Nashville's slaughter house was situated near the market. The ritual slaughtering of meats made it mandatory that the Jewish citizens buy only special cuts of beef, veal and lamb. For the Passover *Matzo*, local Jewry looked to Cincinnati which had established itself as early as 1850 as a Passover food center for the entire Midwest.

After the depression of 1857 America became a country of coffee drinkers. The coffee, parched and ground at home, was increased by the addition of chicory. Local coffee drinkers and bargain hunters were attracted to the advertised merits of the Old Dominion coffee pot. This improved pot boasted a special

123

condenser that prevented the escape of the aroma; it used one-fourth less coffee to produce a perfect cup[56] good to the last drop.

The basic ingredient for the well managed and happy home was a knowledge of bread making. In 1854, a divorce decree issued in Iowa declared the inability to make bread sufficient grounds for divorce.[57] The appearance of a new leavening agent, baking powder, gave impetus to cake and quick bread baking. Early in the decade, bakeries appeared on the local scene. One such bakery sold and delivered twenty-four loaves of bread for one dollar.[58] From neighbors Jewish housewives learned to prepare the favorite Southern dishes of corn pone, turnip greens and sweet potatoes. In exchange they shared their "receipts" for sauerbraten and apple charlotte.

The art of housekeeping and cookery passed from mother to daughter with all of the traditional superstitions concerning food combinations and weather restrictions. The few cook books were exchanged freely; the most widely read sections concerned emetics, paint removing, egg preserving, summer cookery and personal preparation for kitchen duty.[59] To test the heat of an over the following hints were given:

> If hands can be held in oven only as long as 20-35 seconds the oven is a quick oven—if held for 35-45 seconds the oven is moderate—if held for 45-60 seconds the oven is slow.[60]

During the fifties, books on manners for both men and women became popular. Emily Thornwell's, *The Lady's Guide to Perfect Gentility* and Sara J. Hale's, *Happy Home and Good Society,* instructed the reader in the proper manner of chewing food and using cutlery. Only twenty years earlier Nashville had been described as a region of rude manners, where bones were picked with bare hands, knives drawn through the teeth and mocha poured into saucers to expedite cooling.[61] Now folks were learning to eat noiselessly, to avoid sucking, sipping and blowing while eating, and to eat with fork and spoon instead of knife.[62] They learned too, how to correctly set the table with dishes, bottom side up, knives and forks underneath to prevent dust and flies from soiling. In the home where father served the meat and vegetables, and mother the drinks and dessert, refinement and culture were evident.[63]

Improvements in laundry and heating equipment interested the busy housewives who saved their grease and soap scraps to boil with lye and thereby create a clothes and household cleaner. The advertisement of a ten dollar washing machine that "could be operated by a small child with perfect ease"[64] appealed to Rosa Heims, mother of seven children. The use of charcoal as a fuel for the heavy flatirons was probably investigated by Rebecca Powers and Amelia Levy who read that a whole day's ironing could be done with only one cents worth of charcoal.[65] The coal stove was replacing the wood burning stove and the new fuel created interest as it "permitted women to cook without soiling their hands or complexions."[66] The best lump coal to be used in grates or the new "pure air, durable and fire safety" hot air furnace was twenty-one cents a bushel or $5.50 a ton.[67] Nut coal for cooking was thirteen cents a bushel or $3.50 a ton.[68] Unfortunately when the winter demand was the greatest, freezes on the Ohio and Cumberland rivers created shortages.

Equally fascinating was the modern carpet sweeper with revolving fans that sucked up dust and was guaranteed to outlast one thousand brooms.[69] Undoubtedly, the greatest inventions of this era were the safety pin and the sewing machine. Locally, sewing machine dealers had introduced installment selling in a plan to place a machine in every home.

The decade witnessed woman's emergence from the home. On the national scene a growing awareness gave rise to an active struggle for women's rights. The battle of the sexes was aided and abetted by the increasing prosperity. The competition for the favor and affection of a few women in colonial America had early elevated her to a privileged pedestal from which she continued to rule home and husband. Foreign visitors, unanimous in their acclaim of the American woman's beauty, were also unanimous in their disapproval of her vanity, prudery, unhealthfulness and power.[70] I. J. Benjamin, Jewish traveler, stigmatized women with the following comment:

Alexander the great went out with his host to conquer various lands and it is said at last to have reached a land where women ruled; they summoned the men or dismissed them as they pleased and generally regarded them as slaves. I journeyed through several parts of the old world through which Alexander's army went and nowhere did I find a land to which this tale might verify. Accordingly I thought of the whole story as fiction until I found it verified in America.[71]

James Burn, an English workingman, took a dim view of those American women who remained in bed while their husbands made the fires, cooked the breakfast, packed the lunches and did the marketing.[72] *Harper's Monthly* called women the "puppets of the parlor."[73] They were pale due to lack of outdoor exercise. Fashion demanded a delicate gentility; every woman aimed for the clinging vine look.

A false modesty in a straitlaced social system flowered a prudery in women that fostered marital problems, prostitution, illegitimacy and mulatto children. The crowded quarters of many homes exposed young people to child deliveries without acquainting them with the mysteries of birth and conception. Although the Biblical injunction of the ritual bath instructed the young Jewish girl in personal and sexual hygiene, any discussion of sex was taboo. Girls entered the bonds of wedlock innocent of its physical responsibilities. Fidelity in married women was general; the same cannot be said for the men. Prostitution was an acceptable feature of the social scene. In the area of the fourth ward more than one hundred women, in the 1860 census, listed prostitution as their field of employment. The *Nashville Daily News* campaigned editorially for a segregation of these "enchanted ground" areas.[74]

Perhaps the most adverse criticism of American women was aimed at her vanity. *Harper's Weekly* in a poem "Nothing to Wear" said:

> One deserving young lady almost unable
> To survive for the want of a new Russian sable;
> Another confined to the house when it's windier
> Than usual, because her shawl isn't India.

Oh, daughter of Earth; foolish virgins beware
Lest in that upper realm you have nothing to wear.[75]

The hoop skirt invited attention and censure. It created congestion on the sidewalks; it filled the pews at church.[76] As it was vulgar to show contours, corsets were required accessories. The tyrant, fashion, waved his wand, and women followed the dictates of the despot. They read *Godey's* and *Harper's* for fashion hints on morning dresses, walking dresses, manteaus, bonnets, shoes, gloves, jewelry, cosmetics and hair styles. The wedding of the Spanish Eugenie to Napoleon III in 1853 created a new coiffure. The hair was drawn from the face and rolled into a pompadour. Curling hair was accomplished by a handy gadget, the kroll-iron.[77] Mr. Joseph Loisseau, the local hair stylist, sold wigs, curls, braids, puffs and toupees.[78] Young men wore the hair long and oiled it with a cologne perfumed grease.[79]

The visit of the Hungarian Louis Kossuth in 1852 popularized the slouch hat. Men's styles and manners were affected by the nineteen year old Prince of Wales, Edward Albert, who visited America in 1860.[80] Evening attire required swallow tail coat, stiff shirt and bow tie.

Men began to shave the face with the improved Gilchrist razor which required little honing. Usually the side whiskers and mustaches were allowed to attain a luxurious growth. Isaac and Albert, local barbers, operated a shop in the Sewanee House.[81] The skin one loves to touch was achieved in nineteenth century America with the application of a farina or starch powder and the pinching of the cheeks for that rosy glow. The newspapers printed recipes for making tooth paste, hair remover, hair dye, hair restorative, freckle and corn remover. The magic ingredient to be used cost only ten cents. It could also be used as a cement for broken china.[82]

The contemporary scene, as viewed by visiting Europeans, presented a distorted and restricted picture of American life. The time worn adage "Woman's work is never done" continued to describe the world of the majority of nineteenth century women. Despite the many household improvements and increasing prosperity, her world demanded a twenty-four hour alert plus a knowledge of cooking, cleaning, nursing, child psychology and wifely responsibilities. For many Jewish wives there was the added requirement of a proficiency in salesmanship.

The impression that all Americans lived in hotels or boarding houses was misleading. The eight Nashville hotels, catering largely to transients, offered accommodations unparalleled within a widespread area. Among the families listed in the 1860 census at the City Hotel were Mr. and Mrs. Mike Powers. Both the Lusky and the Henry Harris boarding houses attracted a perment Jewish clientele largely among the peddling class. In all likelihood, many families preferred the comfort of well trained servants and bountifully supplied dining rooms.[83]

In an age when eggs sold for five cents a dozen, meal for forty-five cents a bushel and flour for $1.75 a barrel,[84] a laborer's wage of fifty-nine cents a day with board, or eighty-four cents without,[85] was insufficient compensation. The monthly wage for a woman servant averaged $5.12.[86] A study of the 1860 census reveals a preference for foreign servants in the Jewish households. Of the fifteen paid servants in fourteen households, eight were from Ireland, one each from Poland, Prussia and Scotland, three white Americans and one nine year old mulatto girl.[87] The average age of twenty for the paid servants was just half that for the six Jewish owned female slaves whose ages ranged from thirty-two to fifty, averaging forty-one years. Research has revealed the name of only one male servant, a slave, owned by the well known man about town, the unmarried Ben Lyons.[88]

In August 1849, President Zachary Taylor proclaimed the first Friday in August as a day of prayer and fasting to stay the pestilence of cholera that plagued the country. From June 9th to August 1st 1850, it is probable that 500 persons perished from cholera in Nashville.[89] The problems of repeated epidemics, mosquitoes, flies and dirt were not being met by any government agency. Beginning in 1840, repeated efforts to establish a

State Department of Vital Statistics had failed. A City Board of Health was not established until 1866. Eleven years elapsed before the State Board of Health was created. Folks regarded sickness as a visitation from heaven. Each season exacted its toll, in winter lung trouble or "galloping consumption," in summer malaria, typhoid and the illnesses of a child's second summer. Infant mortality was very high. A report of the Nashville Medical Society in 1858 made known that the twenty-eight deaths of children in the month of August 1858 were all for children under two years of age.[90]

Inadequate records make it impossible to list accurately and completely the Jewish dead for the ten year span of 1851 (when cemetery was purchased) to 1861. The known dead included Marx Cline (infant), Rebecca Elsbach (age two), Matilda Harris (15), Barbara Stein (21), Esther Lande (25), Joseph Stein (32), Vogele or Phoebe Heilbon (45), S. K. or S. R. Coleman (63), Emil Heinefeilman (?), Lab. Nassauer (?), Jacob Mitchell (?), Mrs. Isaac Garritson (?).[91]

The median age of the white population in the country in 1860 was 23.56 years.[92] There were still living in the country in 1850, 80,000 octogenarians who had been living when the thirteen colonies became an independent nation in 1776.[93] Although men may have lived longer, it is doubtful that the life span of women was as short as *Harper's Monthly* lamented when it wrote, "It takes two and one-half lives of women to equal one life of man . . . a man of forty-nine marrying a woman of twenty would probably outlive her by one year."[94]

Many of the health problems could be traced to water supply. Nashville had incurred its first debt of $50,000 in 1832 with the establishment of a city water works. By 1861, it was not only one of the few Southern cities with a public water system but it had achieved a reputation for healthfulness in an area of typhus and fevers.[95] Although good water was available, many homes lacked running water, few had bathing facilities and the outside privy was a common sight in the contemporary scene. Drinking water was sold at Sulphur Springs, a popular local bathing establishment where hot or cold showers were available at twenty-five cents a bath or five dollars for the season.[96]

Housewives conducted an endless campaign against roaches, bed-bugs and lice.[97] No home was immune. However, the mandatory health regulations of Jewish law had led to an emphasis on pre-Sabbath and pre-holiday cleaning. No Jewish home in the 1850's would have disregarded the command to cleanse each room, corner to corner, thoroughly and conscientiously of all *Chomas* (unleavened bread) at Passover. If for no other reason than this, a Jewish home received an annual housecleaning.

Poor preparation of food was creating a nation of dypeptics. The South was called an area of the frying pan and the comment, "God sends meat and the devil sends cooks" placed the blame for this commonplace malady on the housewife. Europeans cried that Americans ate too fast and drank too much of that universal drink, ice-water.[98]

Before consulting a doctor, families resorted to home remedies. Neighbors exchanged tested cures of "sulphur, white lead and blue stone" for boils or "biles" as they were prone to say. They pinned their hopes on the curative powers of sassafras, turpentine, licorice, castor-oil, asafetida and goose grease. Free vaccinations, medicine and medical advice were available at the city dispensary, an affiliate of the University of Nashville. Pauper patients, needing hospital care, were sent by the city to Shelby Medical School Hospital for only $1.50 a week.[99] At St. John's Hospital, run by the Sisters of Charity, hospitalization cost three dollars a week with no charge for medicines.[100] The use of the recently discovered anesthetic, chloroform, gave encouragement to the field of surgery.

Newspaper editorials, appealing to the authorities for street improvements, appeared regularly.[101] The ill paved streets, with ruts and crossings out of repair, caused an oftimes impassable situation. The sanitary problem was aggravated by unremoved garbage thrown into the street attracting dogs, cats and hogs.[102] In 1859, when Nashville created the office of civil engineer, $7,452.47 had been spent on the streets.[103] The first street sprinklers, introduced on March 24, 1860, may have increased slightly the elevation of the female crinoline skirts to the joy of the ever present ogling loafer. Although gas lights were installed on the city streets in February 1851, they remained poorly lighted. The Mayor reported 195 gas street lights in 1859.[104] The appearance of the street was definitely not improved by the innumerable telegraph poles.

Nashville streets were frequently used to settle disagreements. Early in the decade, Felix K. Zollicoffer, editor of the *Banner,* and John Marling, editor of the *Union and American,* had an altercation over the site of the new bridge and fought it out in a gunfight on Cherry Street. And again on Cherry Street on October 27, 1859, George Poindexter, editor of the *Union and American,* killed Allen Hall, editor of the *Daily News,* in a political argument. A street brawl involving Jewish participants occurred in May 1857. The fight was precipitated by a law suit involving a Mr. Rice and Mr. Isaac Weill. Rice claimed that Weill had cheated him in a horse and watch trade. In spite of the large delegation that Weill had brought into court, the case was decided against him and he was fined ten dollars. Not satisfied with the court's decision, the case had a second trial on the street conducted by the plaintiff, the defendant and two of the latter's friends, a Mr. Wolf and a Mr. Stein. After some fisticuffs and abusive talk, the police arrived and marched the men back into court, this time Rice was fined[105] and departed a humble and contrite man, we hope.

A study of all the local court records reveal the names of many Jews as both plaintiffs and defendants. The majority of the cases were business suits and naturalizations. Tippling and operating a business without a license or operating on Sunday were the chief misdemeanors. There were several cases of assault and battery.[106] It was an age when the power of the fist was stronger than the law. It also had the power to create a house divided. Mrs. Rosa Coleman and children lived in the same house on south Cherry Street with Mr. and Mrs. H. H. Goldberg and family. On a May Day in 1857 wrangling among the two sets of children soon involved the mothers. Mrs. Coleman slapped Mrs. Goldberg who retaliated with hair pulling.

The subsequent arrest of Mrs. Coleman and the payment of a fine of four dollars[107] restored peace and calm to the crowded household.

"Pretty is as pretty does." "Children should be seen and not heard." These golden maxims dictated the discipline of children in nineteenth century America. In an era when age was regarded as a sign of experience, children were taught to respect the wisdom of elders. The Davidson County census for 1860 counted 2464 white people over fifty years of age in a total white population of 31,056, an average of one in 12.6.[108] Only four persons in the Jewish community had attained these golden years according to the 1860 census. These were Isaac Garritson 64, Michael Schwartz 54, Henry Harris 53, Jonas Heilbon 52. Although Jacob Hyman was not listed in this census record, he too was a member of the Jewish senior citizens. Tombstone markings of birth in 1796 established Hyman's age as 64. Courtesy titles customarily preceded the first name of the person addressed. It was brother Sam, sister Anna, cousin Julia. Jewish family relationships were expressed in the traditional Jewish titles, *bobba* (grandmother), *zeda* (grandfather), *tanta* (aunt) and *onkle* (uncle).

The eternal cry, "the young generation is going to the dogs" was heard throughout the 1850's. Young folks were censured for idleness, thoughtlessness and restlessness.[109] Parental authority came under scrutiny as an accusing finger charged them with extravagant living as "tho gold and silver were to be picked up on the streets."[110] *Harper's Weekly* wrote, "twenty years ago children were lucky if fifty cents was spent on toys . . . now five dollars will hardly purchase one of the tempting tops displayed in the windows."[111] Boys were educated on the streets, the favorite rendezvous being Cedar and Summer Streets.[112] Chasing chickens and hogs, throwing pebbles from housetops at passerbys, flying kites, popping firecrackers in the streets and moving gates at Halloween were the favorite pastimes stamped as nuisances.[113] Parents were further criticized for permitting daughters to appear publicly unchaperoned.[114]

Popular side walk games included hop scotch, I spy, rolling

132

hoops and roller skating.[115] The small children sang and pantomimed "oats, peas, beans and barley grows."[116] In the early half of the decade, children divided off into democrats and whigs. Children of a whig parent proudly sang, "Democrats eat rats and ride on cats."[117] At election time they wore pins for their favorite candidate. Many were wearing small U.S. tags loyally pinned on breasts when President Lincoln called for troops.[118] Boys collected articles and stuffed their pockets for any possible trades with other friendly collectors. One boy's pocket revealed the following contents: sixteen marbles, one top, one oyster shell, two pieces brick, one doughnut, one piece of curry comb, corks, two broken knives, three buckles, a skate strap and a dog eared primer.[119] Girls preferred china dolls, crayons, tapestry needlework and stitching mottoes. Mrs. Martin Sulzbacher taught her daughter Mary the art of sampler making, as she displayed her own handiwork completed in 1831.[120]

A favorite haunt of children was Mr. Shyer's candy shop. For one cent one could purchase a slice of jujube paste or some balsam for chewing. The fancy drops or cocoanut kisses sold for fifteen cents a pound.

It had been a golden era, the prosperous and fabulous fifties. The Jewish community, organized early in the decade by "five families and about eight young men," had shared and taken pride in the progress and growth of Nashville. For everyone there had been occasions of sorrow and joy, but the next four years were to demonstrate that the fifties had truly been a time to live and to laugh.

Heads of Jewish Families Living in Nashville Part
or All of Decade 1851-1861[1]

Aaron, David
Abrahams, Harris
Abrahams, Samuel
Abrahams, Morris
Adler, B.
Adyson, Marks
Attelsohn, Marks

Barnheim, F. W.[2]
Bernstein, Moses
Bloomstein, Jacob
Bloomstein, Louis
Bloomtall, David
Blum, R. D.
Brodie, Samuel
Burnwald, Mire

Citkovitch, Myer
Cline, Nathan
Cohen, Henry
Cohen, Samuel
Cohen, Samuel
Cohn, Joseph
Cohn, Louis
Cohn, M.
Cohn, Morris
Cohn, Simon
Coleman, S. H. or S. K. or S. R.

Delisser, Alexander

Ellis, Jacob
Elsbach, David
Elsbach, Max
Emanuel, Joel

Fisher, Isadore
Flashman, Fred
Flashman, Nathan
Flashman, Phillip
Frank, Isaac

Frankland, Judah[3]
Franklin, Jacob[4]
Franklin, Elias
Franklin, J. K.[4]
Frestenburg, L.
Fry, Joseph
Fry, Louis
Fry, Solomon

Garritson, Isaac
Glashauer, David
Godhelp, Jacob[5]
Godhelp, Sigmund[5]
Goldberg, H. H.
Goldberg, L. D.
Goldstein, I.
Green, Isaac
Green, Samuel
Grund, J.

Hanf, Lewis or Louis
Harris, Hal or Henry[6]
Harris, Henry[6]
Heilbon, Jonas
Heims, Simeon
Heller, E.
Hillman, L.
Hohenstein, Julius[2]
Hyman, Jacob

Isaacs, J.
Iser, Alexander

Jacobs, H.
Jessel, B. A.
Jessel, Henry
Joseph, Isaac
Joseph, Myer

Klein, Alexander
Klein, Bernard

Klein, M.
Kirschbaum, Sam[2]
Kocsiss, Alexander[2]

Lande, Aaron
Lande, Nathan
Lauffer, S.
Lesser, S.
Levi, Marcus
Levick, Samuel
Levinski, Louis
Levy, A.
Levy, J.
Levy, Joseph
Levy, Lehning
Levy, M.
Levy, S.
Levy, Z.
Lewis, Leopold
Lewis, Solomon[7]
Lieberman, S.
Lindheim, A.
Lindoman, A. or L.
Linderman, B.
Lipshar, Myer
Livingston, A.
Livingston, H.
Losminski, Julius
Lusky, Morris or Nallacy
Lusky, Myer
Lusky, Sider
Lyons, E. J.
Lyons, Ben
Lyons, Jacob
Lyons, Lewis
Lyons, Samuel

Marcus, S.
Marcusson, E.
Margolius, Louis
Marks, S.
Marks, T.
Markowiecz, F.
Milius, Wm.

Miller, August
Mitchell, Jacob
Morganstern, Louis or Morris
Myers, Ben
Myers, M. B.

Nassauer, H.
Nassauer, Louis
Nathan, Sinai
Newman, Jacob or A.

Ochs, Julius
Oppenheimer, A. B.
Oppenheimer, Morris

Peixadi, Argolis[2]
Pincus, Isadore
Powers, Louis
Powers, Michael
Powers, Sam

Raphael, Samuel
Rice, M.
Rosenberg, M.
Rosenthar, Nathan
Rymarkiewiez, Joseph

Sandle, Lewis
Schiff, Gustavus
Schlenker, Joseph
Schlessinger, Henry
Schwab, Abram
Schwartz, Michael
Shindler, C.[2]
Shyer, Michael
Shyer, S.
Sigman, Simon
Sobel, D. L.
Sobel, I. M.
Sohn, Louis[8]
Solomon, Jo
Solomon, Joseph
Solomon, Louis
Solomon, Samuel
Spitz, H.
Stein, Isaac

Stein, Joseph
Stein, Morris or Moses
Steinfeld, Nathan
Steinmeier, S.[2]
Sulzbacher, Martin
Swartzenberg, J.

Swartzenberg, L.

Weil, Isaac
Weil, N.
Weiner, Simon
Winter, A.
Wolf, Emanuel

1. As accurate as possible. Differences appear in spelling.

2. Identity as Jewish doubtful.

3. Judah Frankland also spelled Franklin.

4. Jacob and J. K. may be same person.

5. Doubtful if here as early as 1861.

6. One Hal or Henry Harris born in Germany; other Henry Harris born in Austria.

7. Also spelled Solomon Louis.

8. The author thinks Louis Sohn is same as Louis Cohn.

Officers of Congregation Mogen David 1853-1861

	1853-1854	1854-1855	1855-1856
President	Henry Harris	Henry Harris	Abraham Shwab
Vice President	E. Wolf	M. Sulzbacher	E. Wolf
Secretary	L. Hillman	Max Elsbach	Louis Cohn
Treasurer	Max Elsbach	Henry Jessel	S. Nathan
Trustees	E. Franklin, A. Lande, Louis Cohn	Louis Hanf, E. Wolf, M. Rice, E. Franklin	Wm. Milius, T. Marks, B. Linderman, E. Franklin
Warden or Gabah	?	Isaac Garritson	A. Lande
Rabbi	Alexander Iser	Alexander Iser	Alexander Iser

	1856-1857	1857-1858	1858-1859
President	Henry Harris	Henry Harris	Henry Harris
Vice President	?	E. Wolf	E. Wolf
Secretary	David Elsbach	David Elsbach	David Elsbach
Treasurer	?	M. Sulzbacher	S. Nathan
Trustees	?	H. Cohn, S. H. Coleman, S. Levy, L. Bloomstein	S. Louis, S. H. Coleman, M. Sulzbacher, R. D. Blum
Warden or Gabah	?	J. Bloomstein	S. Levy
Rabbi	Alexander Iser	E. Marcusson	E. Marcusson

	1859-1860	1860-1861
President	Henry Harris	L. Levi and Sinai Nathan both listed
Secretary	David Elsbach	David Elsbach
Rabbi	Jonas Heilbon	Jonas Heilbon
Other officers unknown		Unknown

137

Notes to Chapter I

A Time to be Born

1. U. S. Bureau of the Census, Report of the Superintendent of the Seventh Census, 1850, p. 575.
2. *The Jewish Encyclopedia,* Vol. I, p. 492.
3. Peter Wiernik, *History of Jews in America,* p. 149—estimates also given for 1818 as 3000 Jews—1826, 6000 Jews—1840, 15,000 Jews—1848, 50,000 Jews.
4. Samuel Cole Williams, *Early Travels in the Tennessee Country 1540-1800,* p. 120; Lee Friedman, *Pilgrims in a New Land,* p. 239; Albert M. Hyamson, *The Sephardim of England,* p. 159.
5. *The Jewish Encyclopedia,* Vol. XII, p. 104.
6. Stephen B. Weeks, "Tennessee: A Discussion of the Sources of its Population and the Lines of Immigration," *Tennessee Historical Magazine,* Vol. II, p. 249, Dec. 1916; U.S. Bureau of the Census, *A Century of Population Growth from First Census to Twelvth 1790-1900,* p. 121.
7. Jacob R. Marcus, *Early American Jewry,* Vol. II, p. 272.
8. Friedman, *op. cit.,* p. 210.
9. Walter Clark (ed.), *State Records of North Carolina,* Vol. XXVI, lists Elias Coen, Simon Cohon, p. 517—Levi Cone, p. 727, Alexander Levi, Henry Levi, p. 908, Eleazer Levi, Jacob Levi, p. 826—Wm. Cohone, Jacob Cohen, p. 392, Simon Cohon, p. 517.
10. J. Bryan Grimes, *Abstract of North Carolina Wills,* p. 94.
11. *Davidson County Deeds to Property,* Book B, p. 106—William Coen bought land 1790.
12. *Ibid.,* Book W, p. 546—In 1834 an Aaron Cohen also spelled Cohern in same deed purchased property on Market St.
13. *Ibid.,* Book G, p. 321—(Henry Levy purchased property in 1808); Book K, p. 224 (Wm. Levy in 1813); Book L, p. 316 (Thos. Levy); Book 2, p. 424 (James Levy 1822). These were descendants of Alexander and Henry Levi families of Pitt County, N. Carolina. Also marriage license Record of Davidson County lists marriages for Betsy Levy 1810, Thos. Levy 1811, Polly Levy 1814; Jas. Levy 1817, Wm. Levy 1817.
14. H. Enelow, "Influence of Judaism in South," *The South in the Building of the Nation,* Vol. X, p. 559, 1908.
15. Oscar Handlin, *Adventure in Freedom,* p. 64.
16. *Davidson County Deeds to Property,* Book 15, p. 17—deed registered Aug. 12, 1851 shows transfer of property from James C. Owen to Isaac Garritson, Jacob Mitchell and Michael Powers,

Trustees for the Hebrew Benevolent Burial Association called Shield of David. Over 3 acres was purchased for $377.36.

17. T. V. Woodring, *The City Cemetery of Nashville, Tenn., facsimile of original Records of Deaths and Burials.*

18. Felix R. R. Smith, *Alphabetical List of the Dead in the City Cemetery,* p. 10.

19. Gustov Gottheil, "The Position of the Jews in America," *North American Review,* Vol. CXXVI, p. 293.

20. Davidson County, Wills and Inventories, Book 14, 1846-51, pp. 444, 445.

21. Vital Records Congregation Shearith Israel of New York. Also Rabbi Malcolm H. Stern's genealogy of Myers-Hays family in letter to author Sept. 25, 1958.

22. Ira P. Jones, *City of Nashville,* p. 32 estimates Nashville population in 1804 as only 400.

23. U.S. Bureau of the Census, *Population Schedule Inhabitants 1880.* M. B. Myers of Goodlettsville, a brother of Sarah Myers, was listed as 86 years of age—birthplace as Virginia.

24. Jones, *op. cit.,* p. 56.

25. *National Banner and Nashville Whig,* Dec. 23, 1828.

26. *Republican Banner* (Nashville), April 4, 1841.

27. *Davidson County, Circuit Court Minute Book,* 1848, Book Q, page 2.

28. *Ibid.,* 1839 Book K, p. 119.

29. *Davidson County, Criminal Court Minute Book,* Book C (1847-50), p. 174.

30. *Davidson County, Circuit Court Minute Book,* Book M (1842-43), p. 484.

31. *Nashville Whig,* Jan. 15, 1842: *Republican Banner* (Nashville), Feb. 1, 1842.

32. *Nashville Daily Union,* Feb. 17, 1848.

33. *Nashville Gazette,* Nov. 1849 through March 1850.

34. Malcolm H. Stern, genealogist of American Jewish Archives, traced this relationship in a letter to author Oct. 8, 1958.

35. "Excerpts from the Scrap Book of Rev. J. J. Lyons," *Publications American Jewish Historical Society,* Vol. XXVII, pp. 499-500, 1920.

36. Minyan is term describing the quorum of ten men traditionally required for congregational service.

37. A. E. Frankland, "Fragments of History," *Jews' Annual 5650– 1889-1890,* p. 95. The Henry Nathan was undoubtedly Sinai Nathan. The Judah Franklin was probably A. E. Frankland's brother—variance in spelling makes identification difficult.

Notes to Chapter II

A Time to Cast Away

1. *Davidson County, Circuit Court Minute Book*, Book S, 1851, p. 145 states Max Elsback born Waldsdorf April 26, 1829 came to New York in 1845 to Nashville 1849, became citizen 1851. Book T, 1852 p. 28, states David Elsbach born Waldsdorf Feb. 18, 1831, came to New York in 1845, to Nashville 1846, became citizen in 1852.
2. U.S. Bureau of the Census, *Statistical View of the United States,* Being a compendium of Seventh Census, p. 399—census of 1850 gave Nashville population 10,165—foreign born 948.
3. U.S. Bureau of Census, *Population Schedule* 1850, 1860, 1870, reveal place of birth—Minute Books of Davidson County Circuit Court and Minute Books of Davidson County Criminal Court list origin of birth in the applications for citizenship.
4. Robert Ernst, *Immigrant Life in New York City 1825-1863*, p. 8.
5. Mark Wischnitzer, *To Dwell in Safety—a story of Jewish Migration since 1800*, p. 6.
6. Marcus Hansen, *The Atlantic Migration,* 1607-1860, p. 140; Ernst, *op. cit.,* p. 8; Howard M. Sachar, *The Course of Modern Jewish History,* p. 164.
7. *Population Schedule Free Inhabitants 1860.* Phillip and Nathan Flashman, Z. Levy, Isaac Stein, Martin Sulzbacher came from Bavaria.
8. George M. Stephenson, *A History of American Immigration 1826-1864,* p. 77.
9. Bertram W. Korn, *Eventful Years and Experiences,* p. 67; Adolph Korber "Jewish Immigration from Wurttemberg to the United States 1848-1855," *Publications American Jewish Historical Society,* Vol. XLI, No. 3, p. 232, March 1952.
10. Guido Kisch, *In Search of Freedom,* p. 86.
11. Ernst, *op. cit.,* p. 9.
12. Carl Wittke, *Refugees of Revolution,* p. 44.
13. *Davidson County, Circuit Court Minute Book,* 1855, Book V, p. 209. States Louis Cohn, age 28, native of Baden announced his intention of becoming a citizen at Jan. term 1855.
14. Kisch, *op. cit.,* pp. 45-46.
15. S. H. Collins, *Emigrant's Guide to and Description of the United States of America,* p. 66.
16. H. S. Tanner, *View of the Valley of the Mississippi or the Emigrant's and Traveller's Guide to the West,* pp. 209-212.

17. Constantine Belissary, *The Rise of the Industrial Spirit in Tennessee 1865-1885*, p. 162.
18. Thos. D. Clark, *Travels in Old South, A Bibliography*, Vol. III, p. 3.
19. *Davidson County Circuit Court Minute Book*, 1852-53, Book T, p. 17, states Elias Franklin, born Wakrovia 1823, came to United States in 1847.
20. Wittke, *op. cit.*, p. 48.
21. Hyman B. Grinstein, *The Rise of the Jewish Community of New York 1654-1860*, pp. 23, 556.
22. Rolland Abrahams, A letter to author dated July 1958.
23. *Population Schedule Free Inhabitants 1860*. Gives birthplace as England.
24. Wischnitzer, *op. cit.*, p. 6.
25. Eric Hirschler, *Jews from Germany in the United States*, p. 38.
26. Wischnitzer, *op. cit.*, p. 19.
27. Levy and Nassauer Family Records. Information received from Mrs. Emanuel Oury.
28. Abraham V. Goodman (ed.), "A Jewish Peddler's Diary," *American Jewish Archives*, Vol. III, p. 84, June 1951.
29. *Dictionary of American Biography*, Vol. III, p. 615.
30. Ernst, *op. cit.*, pp. 12-13.
31. Carl Wittke, *We Who Built America*, pp. 112,116; Marcus Hansen, *Immigrant in American History*, p. 33; Wittke, *Refugees of Revolution*, p. 52; Guido Kisch, "A Voyage to America Ninety Years Ago," *Publications American Jewish Historical Society*, Vol. XXXV, p. 73; Oscar Handlin, *The Uprooted*, pp. 37-62.
32. U.S. Congress, Senate, *Report of the Select Committee of the Senate of the United States on the Sickness and Mortality on Board Emigrant Ships*, p. 9.
33. *Population Schedule Free Inhabitants 1860*, Joseph listed as born at sea.
34. *Ibid.*
35. *Ibid.*
36. *Ibid.*
37. *Nashville Daily Gazette*, Aug. 4, 1854; I. J. Benjamin, *Three Years in America, 1859-1862*, Vol. I, p. 74, speaks of hundreds waiting at wharf to lure and rob immigrant.
38. Sachar, *op. cit.*, p. 168; Francis Lieber, *Stranger in America*, p. 57.
39. Hirschler, *op. cit.*, p. 38.
40. Abram V. Goodman, *op. cit.*, p. 96.
41. *Population Schedule Free Inhabitants 1860*.
42. *Ibid.*

43. *Davidson County, Circuit Court Minute Book,* 1858, Book W, p. 229, states Solomon Lewis came to United States 1842, at Jan. term 1852 applied for citizenship in Troy, New York, received final papers Davidson County May 1858.

44. *Population Schedule Free Inhabitants 1860.*

45. *Davidson County, Circuit Court Minute Book* 1864, Book Z, states Sigmund Godhelp, born Hesse, Nov. 1836, came Baltimore 1853, Jacob Godhelp born Hesse, April 1838 came Baltimore 1855. Both became citizens Oct. 1864.

46. *Ibid.,* Book Z, says I. Flatu, born Poland, July 1836, came Boston 1854, became citizen Sept. 1864.

47. Abraham's letter, *op. cit.,* "he stowed away on a sailing vessel out of Liverpool bound for the United States, he knew not what port, Put to work aboard ship after he had come out of hiding and the vessel was at sea, he learned he was on his way to New Orleans."

48. *Population Schedule Free Inhabitants 1860.*

49. Sulzbacher Family records. Information received from Mrs. Sigmund Marks and Mrs. Maurice Lowenthal.

50. A. E. Frankland, "Fragments of History," *American Jews' Annual for 5650,* 1889-1890, p. 83.

51. Harold Faulkner, *American Economic History,* p. 317.

52. *Republican Banner* (Nashville), Jan. 11, 1855, reported 14 steamboats at Nashville wharf, great activity.

53. Faulkner, *op. cit.,* p. 317.

54. John A. Kouvenhoven, *Adventure of America, a Pictorial Record,* p. 41; Frederick Law Olmsted, *A Journey through Texas; or a saddle trip on the southwestern Frontier,* pp. 22-37, describes voyage from Louisville to Nashville by steamer in 1856.

55. *Republican Banner,* (Nashville), Jan. 21, 1860. It can not be established that Mr. Cronstine was a resident of Nashville.

56. *An Immigrant of One Hundred Years Ago,* pp. 46,47.

57. Benjamin, *op. cit.,* Vol. I, p. 316.

58. Chas. Henry Ambler, *A History of Transportation in the Ohio Valley,* p. 173.

59. William Chambers, *Things as they are in America,* p. 150.

60. James G. Heller, *As Yesterday When it is Past,* p. 30.

61. Sulzbacher Family Records.

62. David Philipson, "Jewish Pioneers of Ohio Valley," *Publications American Jewish Historical Society,* Vol. VIII, p. 53, 1900.

63. *Davidson County, Marriage Records,* no. 4231, Book II, license for Myer Joseph and Isabella Hyman May 21, 1861.

64. *Nashville Union and American,* June 8, 1875—obituary of Sam Powers.

65. David Turest, "An Appreciation of the Jewish Community in Nashville," *Nashville Y.M.H.A. news.* Dedication no. p. 31, 1924.
66. *Population Schedule 1870.*
67. *Ibid.,* 1860, 1870.
68. *Davidson County Criminal Court Minute Book,* 1847, Book C, p. 89. Henry Harris, born Austria about 1800, came to United States in 1838 to New York, July 1844, made intention to become citizen at circuit court in St. Louis, became a citizen July 1847.
69. *Population Schedule Free Inhabitants 1850.*
70. *Ibid.,* 1860.
71. F. A. Michaux, *Travels to the Westward of the Allegheny Mountains,* p. 247; B. Henry Meyer, *History of Transportation in the United States before 1860,* p. 56.
72. Wm. Darby, *Emigrant's Guide,* p. 43.
73. Ben Cassedy, *History of Louisville,* p. 253.
74. Stanley John Folmsbee, *Sectionalism and Internal Improvement in Tennessee 1796-1845,* p. 247; Orr Collection Mms, Box 2, A letter dated Oct. 22, 1859 from M. H. Hamilton to Sallie said, "I can go to Louisville in 24 hours—railroad is not yet completed."
75. Daughters of American Revolution Magazine, *The American Monthly Magazine,* Vol. II, p. 102, 1854.
76. U.S. Bureau of the Census, *Report of the Superintendent of the Seventh Census,* p. 101.
77. Edwin Huddleston, *Nashville Its [sic] Personality and Progress,* p. 3; Maude Weidner, *Nashville Then and Now* unnumbered; J. C. Guild, *Old Times in Tennessee,* p. 473. These all have accounts of river and rail travel in Nashville.
78. James Ford Rhodes, *History of the United States 1850-1909,* Vol. II, pp. 469, 478; Wm. Chambers, *op. cit.,* pp. 161, 323; Edgar W. Martin, *The Standard of Living,* pp. 248,251, 253; Avard L. Bishop and Albert G. Keller, *Industry and Trade, Historical and Descriptive Account of Their Development in the United States,* p. 321.
79. *Nashville Daily Gazette,* April 28, 1854.
80. *Nashville City and Business Directory, 1860,* pp. 50-55.
81. Henry V. Poor, *Manual of the Railroads of the United States,* p. 27; *Nashville Union and American,* July 7, 1860, stated Tennessee has projected about 1500 miles of railway, has completed until last year 1062 miles.
82. *Population Schedule Free Inhabitants 1860,* listed peddler as occupation of these men.

Notes to Chapter III

A Time to Build Up

1. Torah means the Pentateuch, the first five Books of the Bible, Genesis, Exodus, Leviticus, Numbers, Deuteronomy.
2. The oral and traditional laws that were codified about 500 A.D.
3. Tennessee. Laws, Statutes, etc., *Acts of General Assembly 1853-54*, Chapter 281 p. 555-558, sections 1 through 9 refer to Nashville congregation and list Isaac Garritson, Henry Harris, M. Sulzbacher, Lewis Hanf, Marx Elsbach, A B. Oppenhimer, E. Wolf, A. Lande, L. Sohn, S. Nathan, H. Jessel as incorporators. Sections 10, 11, 12, refer to the Memphis congregation, "Children of Israel" and lists Jos. J. Andrews, Moses Simons, John Walker, D. Levy, Julius Sandec, D. Folz, M. Bornberger, M. Bloom, Joseph Strous, H. Reinach. Act passed March 2, 1854.
4. W. W. Clayton, *History of Davidson County*, p. 342; A. E. Frankland, "Fragments of History," *American Jews' Annual 1889-1890*, p. 95.
5. *Davidson County Deeds to Property*, Book 15, p. 17—deed recorded Aug. 12, 1851.
6. *Ibid.*, Book 17, p. 544—"In a deed recorded November 1853 the land purchased by Hebrew Benevolent Burial Society in 1851 which now has as successors to Isaac Garritson, Jacob Mitchell and Michael Powers, the New trustees A. Lande, Louis Sohn, and E. Franklin and they turn the land over to K. K. Mogen David Board of Trustees, H. Harris, M. Sulzbacher, I. Garritson, H. Jessel, M. Elsbach, Louis Hanf, E. Wolf, E. Franklin and M. Rice."
7. *The Occident*, Vol. XI, p. 187, 1853.
8. Original charter read in Tennessee Legislature. House & Senate Journal list dates of 1st, 2nd, 3rd readings and amendment.
9. Clayton, *op. cit.*, p. 342.
10. *Davidson County, Circuit Court Minute Book*, 1855, Book V, p. 209.
11. *Acts of General Assembly* 1855-56 chapter 43, p. 48, Oct. 31, 1855.
12. *The Occident*, Vol. XV, p. 455, 1857.
13. I. J. Benjamin, *Three Years in America, 1859-1862*, Vol. I, p. 108.
14. *The Israelite*, Vol. VIII, No. 18, p. 142, 1860.
15. *The Asmonean*, Vol. XVI, June, July, August, 1857.
16. *The Occident*, Vol. XV, p. 455, 1857.

17. *Republican Banner,* (Nashville), Sept. 20, 1857.
18. *The Israelite,* Vol. V, No. 16, p. 126, 1858; *Occident,* 1858, Vol. XVI, No. 8, p. 410; *Jewish Messenger,* Vol. IV, No. 11, p. 8, 1858.
19. *Ibid.*
20. Genesis chapter 17, verse 10.
21. *Occident,* Vol. XVI, No. 11, p. 556, 1858.
22. U.S. Bureau of the Census, *Population Schedule* 1860, 1870.
23. *Jewish Messenger,* Vol. VI, No. 17, p. 13, 1859; *The Israelite,* Vol. VI, No. 17, p. 134, 1859.
24. *Ibid., Republican Banner* (Nashville), June 14, 1874 states "Hebrew Sunday School first organized in 1859 by Rev. Mr. Heilbon."
25. Rabbi Alb. Rosenfeld, letter to M. Elsbach, March 12, 1860.
26. Benjamin, *op. cit.,* p. 77-79.
27. *Acts of General Assembly, 1859-1860,* chapter 109, p. 387.
28. Hershel Gower and Jack Allen (ed.), *Pen and Sword, The Life and Journal of Randal W. McGavock,* p. 312.
29. *Occident,* Vol. IX, p. 10, 1851.
30. *Davidson County, Marriage Records,* 1850-1861.
31. *Acts of General Assembly* 1879-80, chapter 98, p. 137, March 1879.
32. *Nashville Daily Gazette,* April 28, 1854.
33. *Davidson County, Wills and Inventories,* 1859-61, no. 18, p. 118.
34. *Acts of General Assembly,* 1859-1860 chapter 95, p. 364.
35. *Jewish Messenger,* Vol. VI, No. 6, p. 44, 1859, *The Israelite,* Vol. VI, No. 15, p. 119, 1859.
36. *Acts of General Assembly,* 1869-1870 chapter 52, p. 476, passed Feb. 25, 1870.
37. *The Israelite,* Vol. X, No. 12, 1863 Delegates from Grand Lodge came to install lodge and officers, Sept. 3, 1863, S. Weil, president; J. M. Druker, Vice president; A. Landsberger, secretary; M. Marburg, treasurer.
38. *Acts of General Assembly,* 1865-66, chapter 4, p. 101.
39. *Ibid.,* 1867-68 chapter 60, p. 123.
40. *The Israelite,* Vol. I, No. 11, p. 85, 1854.
41. *Occident,* Vol. XV, p. 431, 1857; Morris W. Schappes, *A Documentary History of the Jews in the United States 1654-1874,* p. 321.
42. *Occident,* Vol. VII, p. 167, 1850.
43. *The Israelite,* Vol. I, No. 37, pp. 294, 295, 1855.
44. *Nashville Daily Gazette,* May 23, 1854.

45. Harry Simonhoff, *Jewish Notables in America, 1776-1865*, p. 377. Dr. Jacob Marcus thinks Adah Manken was born a Jewess.

46. *Occident*, Vol. XIV, p. 84, 1856; Bernard Illowy, *The Controversial Letters and the Casuistic Decisions of the late Rabbi Bernard Illowy*, with a short history of his life by his son Henry Illoway. pp. 149-154.

47. M. S. Watson, *Nashville during the Civil War*, pp. 2, 8, 9, lists following churches in Nashville at beginning of Civil War, 8 Methodist, 3 Presbyterian, 1 Baptist, 4 Episcopal, 1 Lutheran, 1 Catholic, 1 Jewish, He omitted a second Catholic church.

U.S. Bureau of the Census, Statistics of the United States (including mortality, property, etc.) in 1860, p. 465-466-467 listed for Davidson County 7 Baptist, 4 Christian, 3 Episcopal, 20 Methodist, 5 Presbyterian, 7 Cumberland Presbyterian, 2 Roman Catholic, 3 Union—This list omitted Lutheran and Jewish.

Nashville City and Business Directory, 1860, pp. 8-9, lists 17 white churches, 5 colored.

Notes to Chapter IV

A Time to Plant

1. Mary E. R. Campbell, *Tennessee and the Union 1847-1861*, p. 12.
2. U.S. Bureau of the Census, *Statistics of the United States (including mortality, property, etc.)* in 1860, p. 319.
3. *Ibid.*, p. 312.
4. Hollis Phillip Bacon II, *Historical Geography of Ante-bellum Nashville*, pp. 8-9.
5. *Nashville Daily True Whig*, Jan. 18, 1845.
6. *Nashville Daily Gazette*, Sept. 23, 1857. This article stated further that "Charleston and Louisville each do a heavy business but neither has the amount of capital invested that Nashville has."
7. *Nashville City and Business Directory, 1860-61*, p. 58.
8. I. J. Benjamin, *Three Years in America 1859-1862*, Vol. I, p. 75.
9. The following were peddlers for some part of the decade— Harris Abrahams, Samuel Cohen, Joseph Cohn, Max Edyer (possible Elsbach) Isadore Fisher, Fred Flashman, Lewis Fry, Solomon Fry, David Glashauer, H. H. Goldberg, Isaac Green, Solomon Green, Hal Harris, J. Isaacs, H. Jacobs, Bernard Klein, Myer Lipshar, Myer Lusky, Argolis Peixadi, M. Rosenberg,

Nathan Rosenthar, Lewis Sandle, Michael Schwartz, Joseph Solomon, Marks Adyson, and Marks Attelsohn.

10. U.S. Bureau of the Census, *Population of the United States in 1860*, p. 471.
11. *Nashville Union and American*, Feb. 28, 1854.
12. Quoted in Lee M. Friedman, *Jewish Pioneers and Patriots*, p. 409. Mr. Friedman has an excellent chapter on the Jew in the clothing business.
13. *Nashville Daily Gazette*, Jan. 15, 1857.
14. *Nashville City and Business Directory 1860*, pp. 263, 265.
15. The nine tailors were David Bloomtall, Samuel Green, J. Grund, A. Klein, M. Klein, M. Lusky, H. Myer, Isaac Pincus and Joseph Ruf. Mr. Ruf may not have been Jewish.
16. The three clothing and tailoring establishments were H. Solzberger, H. Shor, M. Sulzbacher. Only religion of Mr. Sulzbacher definitely known as Jewish. The wholesale and retail clothing establishments were Green and Abrams, Simeon Heims, Jessel Bros., Lande and Elsbach, Lande and Schlessinger, M. Levi and Co., S. Levy, J. Levy, Solomon Lewis, Metz and Nathan, L. Powers, Mike Powers, Milius and Wolf. The partnership of Metz and Nathan was a partnership of Christian and Jew. They dissolved about 1857 and each retained one of the two stores that the partnership had owned.
17. E. Heller was listed in the 1850 census as clerk. A. Schwab was both clerk and fruit store owner in 1853 business directory. B. Jessel and H. A. Jessel, brothers were clerks after a brief venture in clothing business in 1853. Later directories list as clerks D. Aaron, S. Lesser, L. or A. Lindheim, Ben Myers, H. Schlessinger, Joseph Solomon, B. Wallman. Listed as bookkeepers were Joe Emanuel and Julius Hohenstein. The 1860 census also listed Joseph Levy as clerk and Nathan Flashman and H. Livingston as laborers.
18. In dry goods and clothing were J. Ellis, Franklin Bros., J. Fry, I. Garritson, H. Harris, Alexander Iser, M. Rice, Isaac Stein.
19. *Nashville Daily Union*, Jan. 5, 1847.
20. *Nashville Daily American*, Aug. 8, 1852.
21. *Republican Banner* (Nashville), Aug. 12, 1853.
22. *Nashville Daily Gazette*, Jan. 6, 1861.
23. *Ibid.*, Aug. 1, 1860.
24. *Nashville Union and American*, June 8, 1875. The obituary of Sam Powers gave much family information.
25. *Nashville True Whig*, Sept. 26, 1854.
26. *Ibid.*, Oct. 31, 1849; *Nashville Daily Gazette*, Nov. 17, 1849.

27. *Nashville Daily Gazette,* Mar. 26, 1850.
28. *Nashville True Whig,* Nov. 16, 1854.
29. *Republican Banner* (Nashville), May 7, 1857.
30. *Nashville Daily Gazette,* Jan. 17, 1854; *Nashville True Whig,* Sept. 15, 1854.
31. *Nashville City and Business Directory* 1853-54, pp. 38, 39. 1855-56, p. 69; 1857-58, p. 126; 1859, p. 95.
32. *U.S. Bureau of the Census, Population Schedule Free Inhabitants 1860.* Mr. Isaac Stein owned much property.
33. Information received from sons of Mr. Joseph Stein.
34. Bacon, *op. cit.,* p. 183.
35. *Nashville Daily American,* May 21, 1857.
36. Bacon, *op. cit.,* p. 181.
37. *Nashville True Whig,* March 1, 1854.
38. Emilie Marguerite Cowell, *The Cowells in America,* ed. M. Willson Disher, pp. 96-97.
39. *Nashville True Whig,* Feb. 25, 1851.
40. Lewis Cecil Gray, *History of Agriculture in the Southern United States to 1860,* Vol. II, pp. 97-98.
41. *Nashville Daily Gazette,* Jan. 14, 1857.
42. Freeman Hunt, *Worth and Wealth,* p. 104.
43. *Nashville Daily Gazette,* Jan. 14, 1855.
44. *Campbell, op. cit.,* 1857-58, p. 9.
45. *Ibid.,* p. 14.
46. *Ibid.,* p. 10.
47. *Asmonean,* Vol. VII, No. 14, p. 158, 1855.
48. R. Turner Wilcox, *The Mode in Footwear,* p. 139.
49. Local grocers were Sam Abrahams, L. Bloomstein, J. Bloomstein, Morris Lusky, Morris Abrahams, Joseph Rymarkiewicz, Simon Sigman, Louis Solomon, M. Sulzbacher.
50. Mary Woods, *Memories and Recollections of Mary Woods,* p. 3, Miss Woods wrote that stalls at market house opened at sunrise.
51. *Nashville Daily Gazette,* Jan. 6, 1858; Feb. 3, 1858.
52. *Population Schedule Free Inhabitants 1860.* Mr. Laufer was listed as cattle dealer in census but an earlier business directory lists him as a merchant. The author is doubtful of religion of C. Shindler listed in 1860 census as a butcher.
53. David Turest, "An Appreciation of the Jewish Community in Nashville," *Nashville Y.M.H.A. News,* Dedication No. p. 31, 1924.
54. *The Israelite,* Vol. VI, No. 41, p. 326.
55. *Nashville Daily Gazette,* Jan. 21, 1861; Feb. 20, 1861.

56. *Nashville City and Business Directory*, 1860, p. 128; *Population Schedule Free Inhabitants 1860* lists Nathan Cline as a dealer in liquor.

57. *Nashville Daily Gazette*, July 31, 1852.

58. *Ibid.*, Sept. 3, 1857.

59. *Ibid.*, Sept. 20, 1857.

60. *Ibid.* Jan. 17, 1855; April 30, 1855. Nathan Steinfeld and M. Burnwald were listed as cigar makers in *Population Schedule Free Inhabitants 1860*. The author can not establish as Jewish, B. H. Barkhorn owner of a cigar store on Deadrick Street in 1855.

61. *First Annual Exhibition of the Mechanics Institute of Tennessee*, p. 3.

62. *Nashville Daily Gazette*, Oct. 7, 1857.

63. Constantine J. Belissary, *The Rise of the Industrial Spirit in Tennessee 1865-1885*, p. 19.

64. Constantine J. Belissary "Tennessee and Immigration 1865-1880,"*Tennessee Historical Quarterly*, Vol VII, No. 3, p. 230 Sept. 1948.

65. E. Steadman, *A Brief Treatise on Manufacture in the South*, pp. 19-20.

66. First American National Bank, *Firsts in Nashville*, p. 13.

67. *Republican Banner* (Nashville), May 31, 1856.

68. *Ibid.*, Feb. 15, 1860.

69. *Nashville Daily Gazette*, Jan. 6, 1857; Feb. 21, 1857; Jan. 5, 1860; Jan. 20, 1860; *Nashville Daily American*, Jan. 19, 1854; *Nashville Union and American*, Feb. 14, 1860.

70. Bacon, *op. cit.*, p. 11.

71. *Nashville Daily Gazette*, Jan. 14, 1849.

72. The religious affiliations of F. W. Barnheim, A. Hirschfield and Abe Joseph, all jewelers, have not been established.

73. *Nashville Daily Gazette*, May 7, 1858.

74. Gerald W. Johnson, *An Honorable Titan*, p. 15.

75. *Nashville Daily Gazette*, July 31, 1852.

76. *Population Schedule Free Inhabitants 1860*.

77. A. E. Frankland, "Fragments of History," *American Jews' Annual 5650*, p. 93.

78. Edgar W. Martin, *The Standard of Living in 1860*, p. 223.

79. Ruth Irene Jones, "Hot Springs: Ante-Bellum Watering Place," *Arkansas Historical Quarterly*, Vol. XIV, pp. 19,21, 1955.

80. *The Jewish Encyclopedia*, Vol. II, p. 113; Frankland, *op. cit.*, pp. 95-96. Mr. Frankland in a comment on the Jews of Arkansas wrote that Jacob Mitchell was involved for many years in

litigation with the U.S. government over ownership of Hot Springs which was finally awarded to the government to the "disappointment of the Mitchell family."

81. *Nashville Union and American,* Mar. 9, 1856.
82. *Nashville Daily Gazette,* Jan. 3, 1861; W. W. Clayton, *History of Davidson County,* p. 279.
83. *Republican Banner* (Nashville) April 5, 1861.
84. *Nashville Daily Gazette,* Jan. 15, 1854.
85. *Ibid.,* Jan. 2, 1861.
86. Benjamin, *op. cit.,* p. 98.
87. *Nashville Union and American,* July 24, 1856.
88. *Republican Banner* (Nashville), Dec. 24, 1859.
89. Michael Kraus, *The United States to 1865,* p. 463.
90. *Ibid.*
91. *Nashville Daily Gazette,* Jan. 14, 1855.
92. *Ibid.,* Sept. 29, 1857.
93. Philip Sheldon Foner, *Business and Slavery; the New York Merchants and the Irrepressible Conflict,* p. 144.
94. *Nashville Daily Gazette,* Oct. 30, 1857.
95. *Republican Banner* (Nashville), Oct. 7, 1860.
96. *Nashville Union and American,* March 7, 1860.
97. Disher, *op. cit.,* p. 96.
98. *Republican Banner* (Nashville) April 3, 1861.
99. *Davidson County Chancery Court Minutes,* Book I 1860 to Book L 1866.

Notes to Chapter V

A Time to Speak

1. Mr. Jacob Isaacs a member of the U.S. Congress from Tennessee about 1830 was listed in the *Universal Jewish Encyclopedia,* Vol. X, p. 198 as a Jew. There is no verification for this statement, Mr. Isaacs was probably of Penn-Dutch Protestant descent.
2. U.S. Bureau of the Census, *Statistical View of the United States; Being a Compendium of the Seventh Census,* pp. 397, 399. The population of Nashville in 1850 was 10,165—of these there were 511 free blocks and 2,028 slaves, of the 948 of foreign birth, 208 were Germans.
3. The author has established by means of census records of 1850, deeds to property, death records and circuit and criminals court records the following as citizens in 1850—I. H. Goldstein, native of North Carolina, Isaac Joseph, native of South Carolina,

Louis Hanf, Henry Harris, I. Garritson, Louis Powers, Michael Powers and M. Rice. Although Jacob Mitchell arrived in Arkansas in 1830's and M. Sulzbacher's arrived in Cincinnati about 1840 they can not be traced as Nashville residents until 1851. Status of E. Wolf is also unknown.

4. The author has established dates of citizenship for the following in the 1850-60 decade:

Aaron, David, 1858, *Circuit Court Minutes, Book W*, p. 403.
Bloomstein, Louis, 1858, *Criminal Court Minute Book F*, p. 330.
Citkovitch, Myer, 1857, *Criminal Court Minute Book E*, p. 57.
Cline, Nathan, 1857, *Criminal Court Minute Book Book E*, p. 532.
Cohn, Louis, 1855, *Circuit Court Minute Book Book V*, p. 209.
Ellis, Jacob, 1860, *Circuit Court Minute Book X*, p. 57.
Elsbach, David, 1852, *Circuit Court Minute Book T*, p. 28.
Elsbach, Max, 1851, *Circuit Court Minute Books*, p. 145.
Fleshman, Nathan, 1859, *Criminal Court Minute Book G*, p. 333.
Franklin, E., 1852, *Circuit Court Minute Book T*, p. 17.
Franklin or Frankland, Jacob, 1855, *Circuit Court Minute Book V*, p. 419.
Green, Isaac, 1860, *Criminal Court Minute Book H*, p. 119.
Harris, Henry, 1860, *Criminal Court Minute Book H*, p. 21.
Klein, Alexander, 1859, *Circuit Court Minute Book W*, p. 193.
Lande, A., 1853, *Circuit Court Minute Book T*, p. 214.
Lewis, Leopold, 1856, *Circuit Court Minute Book V*, p. 92.
Lewis, Solomon, 1858, *Circuit Court Minute Book W*, p. 229.
Margolius, Louis, 1859, *Circuit Court Minute Book W*, p. 101.
Nathan, Sinai, 1856, *Criminal Court Minute Book E*, p. 359.
Schlenker, Joseph, 1859, *Criminal Court Minute Book G*, p. 331.
Shyer, S., 1859, *Circuit Court Minute Book W*, p. 193.
Sobel, I. M., 1858, *Circuit Court Minute Book W*, p. 230.

The Henry Harris listed above is not to be confused with Henry Harris (note 2) who received his citizenship 1847, *Criminal Court Minute Book*, p. 89. It must be remembered that many of Nashville's newcomers received their first and second papers elsewhere.

5. James Ford Rhodes, *History of the United States from the Compromise of 1850*, Vol. II, p. 460.
6. Mary E. R. Campbell, *Tennessee and the Union 1847-1860*, p. 12. Mrs. Campbell wrote that one could withstand the long speeches in anticipation of the free barbecue.
7. Hershel Gower and Jack Allen (ed.), *Pen and Sword, The Life and Journal of Randal W. McGavock*, p. 421.

8. *Nashville Daily Gazette,* August 20, 1858.

9. *Ibid.* July 6, 1860.

10. *Ibid.* Sept. 20, 1854. States 400,000 newspapers and periodicals in country.

11. Frederika Bremer, *America of the Fifties: Letters of Frederika Bremer,* pp. 252-253. Mrs. Bremer wrote that one might imagine the Union was being torn to shreds and every citizen being attacked by his neighbor in this political game or race. Francis Lieber, *The Stranger in America,* p. 23. Mr. Lieber wrote that placards at voting places said if candidate of other ticket elected, the commonwealth would perish and liberty, happiness and national honor be lost.

12. *Nashville, Board of Aldermen Minutes* 1857-1860, pp. 10,11, 120. Mr. Isaac Garritson protested assessment of his property Feb. 11, 1858, *Ibid.* p. 58.

13. *Nashville Union and American,* June 16, 1855; Aug. 4, 1859. In 1856 the question of six months residency was referred to a committee from both political parties and decision was made that the six months residency requirements should be prior to obtaining citizenship papers. Gower and Allen *op. cit.,* p. 247, Randal McGavock presented an Irishman to vote at two polls on Aug. 6, 1857. At one he was refused because papers were not six months old and "majority of judges were Know Nothings," at second place he was permitted to vote as papers were final.

14. *Republican Banner* (Nashville), Nov. 6, 1860.

15. Statistical View of Seventh Census, pp. 156-157; Campbell, *op. cit.,* p. 8.

16. The Nashville dailies were *Nashville Daily Gazette, Nashville News, Nashville Patriot, Nashville Union and American,* and *Republican Banner.* During the 1850's papers were sometimes titled differently.

17. *Tennessee House Journal* 1853, pp. 176-177, cited in Robert H. White, *Messages of the Governors of Tennessee* 1845-1857, Vol. IV, p. 604.

18. *Nashville Union and American,* April 28, 1855; June 16, 1855; July 21, 1855. This democratic paper supported Andrew Johnson and branded Philip S. White, a lecturing temperance worker, as a member of the Know Nothing party.

19. J. J. Peres, Rev., "Temperance Among Israelites," *The Occident,* Vol. XVII, pp. 63-64, 1859.

20. White, *op. cit.,* Vol. V, p. 175.

21. *Ibid.,* p. 174.

22. *Nashville Minutes of Board of Aldermen* 1854-1857, p. 302. The value of taxable slaves was $1,200,410.
23. *Ibid.*, 1857-1860, pp. 17,23.
24. *Ibid.*, p. 63.
25. Campbell, *op. cit.*, p. 63.
26. *Annual Report of the American and Foreign Anti-Slavery Society*, pp. 114-115 cited in Bertram W. Korn, *American Jewry and the Civil War*, p. 15.
27. U.S. Bureau of the Census, *Population Schedule of Slave Inhabitants 1860.* The following were owners of slaves.

Owner	Number	Age	Sex	Color
S. Nathan	1	32	F	Black
Martin Sulzbacher	1	50	F	Black
Simon Cohn	1	36	F	Mulatto
M. B. Myers	1	35	F	Black
Alexander Iser	1	50	F	Black
Louis Powers	1	42	F	Black
Ben Lyons	1	18	M	Black

28. *Republican Banner* (Nashville), Nov. 1, 1861.
29. *Nashville Daily Gazette*, Oct. 13, 1860. This paper declared itself to be a neutral paper and warned that sectional madmen were throwing the country into war.
30. *Nashville Union and American,* Oct. 23, 1860; Nov. 1, 1860.
31. *Republican Banner* (Nashville), Oct. 14, 1860.
32. *Ibid.* Oct. 12, 1860.
33. Constantine Belissary, *Tennessee and Immigration* 1865-1880, pp. 162, 163.
34. U.S. Bureau of the Census, *Population of the United States in 1860*, pp. 466, 467, 468, 470. Population Tennessee, whites 826,782, free black 7,300, slave 275,719, total 1,109,801—white native 805,556, foreign 21,226. Population Davidson County, white 31,056, free black 1,205, slave 14,790, total 47,055 white native 26,674, foreign 4,382 white & 4 black. Population Nashville 13,043 white, 719 free black, 3,226 slave total 16,988.
35. Mary de Lourdes Gohrmann, sister, *Political Nativism in Tennessee to 1860*, p. 93.
36. Robert Loren Hargis, *The Know Nothing Party in Tennessee*, p. 5.
37. *Nashville Daily Gazette*, Sept. 20, 1854.
38. *Ibid.* July 6, 1854.
39. U.S. Bureau of the Census, *Population Schedule Free Inhabitants 1850.*

153

40. Davidson County election returns showed majority votes for Whig or American party. Nominees for governor in 1849, 1851, 1853, 1855, 1857. The county also had majority returns for Whig presidential nominee Scott in 1852 and American or Know Nothing nominee Fillmore in 1856.

41. Gower and Allen, *op. cit.*, p. 338 Randal McGavock wrote in his diary that Know Nothing thoroughly organized and numbered some of best and oldest democrats of the country.

42. Philip M. Hamer (ed.) *Tennessee—A History,* vol. 1, p. 496, The democrats expecting to win had not attended the polls.

43. *Nashville Daily Gazette,* Sept. 19, 1854. The Turnverein did not appear on the local scene until later, one was chartered Oct. 24, 1865—Tenn. Laws, Statutes, etc., Acts of General Assembly 1865-66, ch. 3, sec. 1 p. 99.

44. *Nashville Union and American,* Sept. 24, 1854, Jan. 7, 1855, April 22, 1855, May 5, 1855, May 23, 1855. This paper declared no more foreigners or Catholics in country now than when declaration of independence was signed, "Americans were once all foreigners."

45. Tenn. Governor, *Messages of the Governors of Tennessee* by Robert H. White, Vol. IV, p. 616.

46. *Ibid.* p. 626.

47. *Nashville Union and American,* May 3, 1855.

48. *Nashville Patriot,* July 26, 1856.

49. *Nashville Union and American,* July 30, 1856.

50. *Nashville Patriot,* July 31, 1856.

51. *Nashville Union and American,* July 31, 1856.

52. *Nashville Daily Gazette,* July 31, 1856.

53. *The Israelite,* Vol. 3, No. 8, p. 62.

Notes to Chapter VI

A Time to Seek

1. W. K. Bowling M.D., *An Oration Pronounced Upon the Occasion of the Laying of the Cornerstone of the Nashville High School,* p. 8.

2. Edgar W. Martin, *The Standard of Living in 1860,* p. 297.

3. Herbert Henry Todd, *The History of Educational Legislation in Tennessee to 1860,* p. 24.

4. Harold E. Ward, *Academy Education in Tennessee Prior to 1861,* pp. 4,6.

5. Robert Hiram White, *Development of the Tennessee Educational Organization 1796-1929,* pp. 39-77.

No provisions had been made for school lands when Tennessee became a state. The first legislation between Federal government, North Carolina and Tennessee in 1806 did not include the older settled areas. School legislation to provide sufficient funds was not enacted until regime of Andrew Johnson in 1854.

6. R. C. Hawkins, "Old Resident Describes Nashville Business Section of Civil War Days," *Nashville Banner*, May 20, 1928.

   Mr. Hawkins, born in Nashville in 1845, attended a private school at Central Baptist Church, 633 Cherry Street and commented that boys from Central would call after boys who attended the free Trimble School, "Hey you trundle-bed trash." This always provoked a fight.

7. U.S. Bureau of the Census, *Statistical View of the United States; Being a compendium of the Seventh census*, p. 303.

   There were only 1208 pupils in public schools in Davidson county in 1850. U.S. Bureau of the Census, *Seventh Census of the United States, 1850*, p. 579, states Davidson County had 29 private schools, academies and colleges and 6337 pupils. *Nashville Whig*, July 11, 1821 advertised first common school in Nashville which opened September 11, 1821, conducted by Mr. Joseph Herron who taught reading, writing, English, grammar, bookkeeping, geography, $3 tuition.

8. *Nashville, Revised Laws of City 1806-1855*, Vol. II, p. 172.

9. Alfred Hume, *Report on the Subject of Public Schools in the city of Nashville made to Board of Mayor and Aldermen;* J. Emerick Nagy Collection, Box 32, *Minute Books of Board of Education*, p. 1. A board of education was permanently organized in Fall of 1854. Joshua Pearl of Memphis was elected Superintendent of schools at an annual salary of $2500.

10. The seventh and eighth census records indicate ages and birthplaces of these children. A Matilda Harris was listed as a student in the primary department of Nashville Ladies College in 1854. No proof can be established that this Matilda was a daughter of Henry and Esther Harris, Jewish residents of Nashville.

11. Nashville Board of Education, *First Report of the Board of Education and Superintendent of Schools of Nashville*, p. 6.

12. *Ibid.*

13. *Third Report of Board of Education and Superintendent of Schools*, p. 7. There are many discrepancies in figures for the number of pupils in 1860. *Nashville City and Business Directory 1860*, says 2000 pupils; *Republican Banner*, October 16, 1860 lists 1640; *Nashville Patriot*, January 27, 1860 claims

1892. There are also discrepancies in names of schools. Nagy, *op. cit.*, pp. 143-145 fails to name the rented room at Primitive Baptist church also called Hard Side Baptist School.

14. All of these children appeared in the 1860 census for Nashville—none were in 1850 census.

15. G. W. Hubbard, *A History of the Colored Schools of Nashville, Tennessee*, p. 4.

16. Nashville Board of Education, *Rules for the Government of the Free Schools of the City of Nashville*, pp. 1-7. This pamphlet names subjects to be taught in all departments.

17. Nagy, *op. cit.*, pp. 72-73; *Nashville Union and American*, Jan. 18, 1857; *Nashville Patriot*, May 2, 1857.

18. *Nashville Patriot*, Feb. 10, 1857.

19. William Mulkey, *The Orthographical Spelling Book*, pp. 9-10.

20. *Nashville Patriot*, Feb. 23, 1857.

21. Edgar W. Knight, *Public Education in the South*, p. 290.

22. Nagy, *op. cit.*, p. 46.

23. *Nashville Patriot*, August 28, 1858. Eighty-one boys and eighty girls suspended for irregular attendance, two boys suspended for truancy, one girl for obstinancy, six girls for marriage.

24. S. W. Bransford, "A letter to Editor," *Nashville Banner*, Nov. 18, 1931. Mr. Bransford was a student in first city public school.

25. I. J. Benjamin, *Three Years in America*, Vol. I, p. 86.

26. John C. Cooke, "Memories of Days of Long Ago Recalled," *Nashville Banner*, September 6, 1931. There were 137 more ornamental students than boarding students.

27. *Nashville Union and American*, March 18, 1855.

28. W. W. Clayton, *History of Davidson County*, p. 257.

29. Martin, *op. cit.*, p. 302.

30. Tenn. Laws, Statutes, etc., *Acts of General Assembly 1848*, ch. 91, sec. 15, p. 144, Jan. 24, 1848.

31. *Republican Banner (Nashville)*, Oct. 12, 1860.

32. *Nashville Union and American*, Feb. 22, 1859.

33. *Ibid.*, Nov. 12, 1852.

34. *Ibid.*, Sept. 15, 1853.

35. *Nashville Patriot*, Sept. 17, 1858. Oct. 1, 1860. St. Mauir Stuart had special classes for young business men.

36. *Catalogue of the University of Nashville 1859-1860*, p. 16.

37. *Nashville Patriot*, Sept. 7, 1859; Francis Garvin Davenport, *Cultural Life in Nashville 1850-1860*, pp. 51-61. Mr. Davenport has an excellent account of University of Nashville. Students in the literary department were given permission to have fire-arms and attendance of servants. Board was available for all students at three to four dollars a week.

38. *Nashville Union and American,* Jan. 26, 1859. An advertisement announced Mr. Dolbear as a teacher of writing. The three commercial colleges were Southern Commercial, Carney's and Nashville Commercial College which also taught surveying, engineering and architectural drawing.
39. *Nashville Whig,* Dec. 6, 1842.
40. Martin, *op. cit.,* p. 330.
41. *Nashville Patriot,* Sept. 14, 1859. A reprint.
42. *Nashville Union and American,* Jan. 1, 1854; Feb. 17, 1854.
43. *Nashville Daily American,* Jan. 8, 1852.
44. *Nashville Patriot,* Jan. 6, 1857.
45. *Nashville Union and American,* March 13, 1855.
46. *Ibid.,* Dec. 27, 1853; *Nashville Daily Gazette,* July 30, 1852. *Nashville Patriot,* Jan. 1, 1857; Aug. 20, 1859.
47. Nagy, *op. cit.,* p. 114, Sept. 28, 1859.
48. Warren S. Tryon, "The Publications of Tichenor and Fields in the South 1840-1865," *The Journal of Southern History* Vol. XIV, p. 305, Aug. 1948.
49. *Ibid.*
50. *Nashville City and Business Directory,* 1859, p. 7.
51. Martin, *op. cit.,* p. 324.
52. *Nashville City and Business Directory* 1860, p. 45.
53. *First Annual Exhibition of the Mechanics Institute of Tennessee,* pp. 5,7.
54. *Nashville City and Business Directory* 1860, p. 81.
55. *Ibid.,* p. 45; Davenport, *op. cit.,* p. 228.
56. *Nashville City and Business Directory* 1860, p. 40-41.
57. *Ibid.,* p. 43.
58. Douglas Anderson, "Negro Slavery and the White Man's Genius," *Nashville American,* Oct. 16, 1904.
59. Frederick Law Olmsted, *A Journey Through Texas; or a Saddle Trip on the Southwestern Frontier,* p. 35.
60. Davenport, *op. cit.,* p. 230.
61. *Nashville Daily American,* Nov. 4, 1851.
62. The Redelsheimer family came to Nashville from Macon, Ga. during period of Civil War bringing with them a family prayer book published in Roedelsheim, Germany in 1819. Dr. Arthur Redelsheimer of San Diego, Calif. is the present owner of book. The author is indebted to Mrs. Stanley Simm of Nashville for this information.
63. *Nashville Union and American,* Aug. 15, 1859. A woman in Trumbull County, Ohio, gave birth to 8 children within one day.
64. *Ibid.,* Jan. 26, 1854. This paper advocated passage of a bill before legislature to protect property of women and children.

65. *Republican Banner* (Nashville), March 27, 1861.

66. The Adelphi Theater opened on Cherry Street July 1, 1850, and existed as Bijou Theater until recently razed for the Capitol Hill Redevelopment.

67. Davenport, *op. cit.*, pp. 189-195; *Nashville Daily Gazette,* April 2, 1851. This paper expressed disappointment in the great Jenny, said she lacked sentiment.

68. C. G. Rosenberg, *Jenny Lind in America,* p. 192.

69. *Republican Banner* (Nashville), May 27, 1852.

70. Liston Lewis, "Things Theatric in Nashville," *Nashville Banner,* Nov. 26, 1933, Mr. Lewis wrote that 300 subscribers had been obtained for the opera. The first night's production was Lucia de Lammermoor.

71. *Nashville Daily Gazette,* May 30, 1854; *Nashville Union and American,* May 28, 1854. The latter paper was concerned with opera company's opinion of Nashville and wrote, "Let us conclude with Hamlet that we had better have a bad epitaph after death than their ill repute while we live."

72. Kenneth Daniel Rose Papers, *Pioneer Nashville Its Songs and Tunes,* Vol. II, p. 72.

73. Lewis, *op. cit.*, Nov. 26, 1933.

74. *Nashville Union and American,* April 10-11-12, 1854; May 9, 1854; *Republican Banner* (Nashville) Dec. 28, 1855; *Nashville Daily American,* Dec. 2, 1851.

75. *Nashville Patriot,* March 9, 1859.

76. James E. Murdoch, *The Stage or Recollection of Actors and Acting,* pp. 285-289; *Nashville Union and American,* Jan. 22, 1858. The author can not establish if this date when both Murdoch and Menken played in Nashville is date of Menken's unforgettable Lady Macbeth.

77. *Nashville Union and American,* Nov. 27, 1854; *Republican Banner* (Nashville), Dec. 3, 1855.

78. Emilie Marguerite Cowell, *The Cowells in America,* ed. M. Willson Disher, pp. 43-44.

79. *Nashville Daily Gazette,* April 16, 1853; Dec. 9, 1855; *Nashville Union and American,* May 28, 1854; Dec. 10, 1857; *Nashville Daily News,* Oct. 29, 1859.

80. *Nashville Union and American,* Feb. 3, 1854.

81. *Ibid.*, Jan. 26, 1859; *Nashville Daily Gazette,* April 3, 1857; Feb. 26, 1856; *Nashville Patriot,* Feb. 27, 1857.

82. Robertson Association, *Constitution of Robertson Association of City of Nashville,* p. 5.

83. *Nashville Patriot,* Feb. 17, 1857; March 12, 1857.

84. *Nashville Union and American,* April 29, 1857; Dec. 29, 1857.

85. *Nashville Daily Gazette,* Nov. 12, 1859.

86. *Republican Banner* (Nashville), Feb. 25, 1858; *Nashville Daily News,* March 5, 1859.

Notes to Chapter VII

A Time to Laugh

1. *Nashville Daily Gazette,* July 7, 1860. One of earliest notices to reduce the working day was made in summer of 1860 when stores closed at 6 P.M. from July 1 to Sept. 1 to permit some opportunity for relaxation. N. Cline & Co. was a signer.

2. *Nashville Patriot,* Aug. 7, 1858; Nov. 1, 1858; *Nashville Union and American,* Jan. 9, 1859; *Nashville Daily Gazette,* Feb. 20, 1861.

3. *Nashville Patriot,* July 24, 1860; John T. S. Fall, *The Excursion of the Fourth Day of July 1860—84th Anniversary of the Declaration of Independence, A Heroic Poem in 9 Cantos.*

4. *Nashville Patriot,* July 10, 1858.

5. *Nashville Daily Gazette,* Oct. 12, 1857.

6. Hershel Gower and Jack Allen (ed.), *Pen and Sword, The Life and Journal of Randal W. McGavock,* p. 312. Mr. McGavock commented on lack of resort places adding, "One dislikes the idea of visiting."

7. *Nashville Daily Gazette,* Feb. 20, 1861.

8. *Ibid.,* Oct. 17, 1857.

9. *Nashville Union and American,* March 1, 1855.

10. U.S., Bureau of the census *Statistics of the United States (including mortality, property, etc.,) in 1860,* p. 312. Figures are not available for Nashville. Davidson county property was valued at $84,898,053.

11. *The Israelite,* Vol. VI, No. 17, p. 134. This was an account of death of S. H. Coleman at Red Boiling Springs on Sept. 18, 1859.

12. *Nashville Daily Gazette,* July 31, 1857.

13. Frederic L. Paxson, "The Rise of Sports," *The Mississippi Valley Historical Review,* Sept. 1917, Vol. IV, No. 2, p. 151.

14. *Nashville Union and American,* March 7, 1860.

15. *American Jews' Annual* 5646—1885-86, p. 114. Aaron won in New Orleans Apr. 11, 1857 and in Canada Sept. 29, 1857.

16. *Nashville Patriot,* Sept. 1, 1860.

17. Eric Bender, *Tickets to Fortune,* pp. 109-126.

18. *Nashville Daily Gazette,* Jan. 3, 1857; Jan. 19, 1855; Jan. 30, 1855.

19. *Nashville Daily News,* July 2, 1858.
20. Phyllis Elizabeth Hahn, *German Settlers in Nashville Tennessee,* p. 56; Joseph Tant MacPherson, Jr., *Nashville's German Element 1850-1870,* p. 57.
21. *Nashville Daily News,* Aug. 14, 1859.
22. *Ibid.,* April 11, 1858.
23. Hahn, *op. cit.,* p. 54; MacPherson, *op. cit.,* p. 92.
24. *Nashville Daily Gazette,* Sept. 19, 1854.
25. *Tenn. Laws, Statutes, etc., Acts of General Assembly* 1865-66, ch. 3, sec. 1, p. 99, Oct. 24, 1865. Hahn, *op. cit.,* p. 55 says Turn Verein organized Oct. 24, 1854. The author thinks this is an error.
26. *Nashville Daily Gazette,* July 29, 1860.
27. *Nashville Daily American,* Nov. 14, 1851; Dec. 31, 1851.
28. *Nashville City and Business Directory,* 1860-1861, pp. 77-78.
29. Randal W. McGavock, *Communication from His Honor the Mayor—transmitted to the City Council of Nashville Tennessee Sept. 30, 1859,* p. 10.
30. *Nashville Patriot,* Aug. 17, 1859; Sept. 12, 1859.
31. *Nashville Daily Gazette,* Sept. 11, 1866. The obituary of Judah Frankland stated he had been a volunteer fireman of company 3.
32. *Republican Banner* (Nashville), May 17, 1860. Ben Lyons threw open his billiard parlor to visiting firemen as he was an old fireman himself.
33. *Nashville Daily News,* April 11, 1858.
34. *Nashville Union and American,* April 8, 1875.
35. *New York City Bureau of Municipal Archives and Records.* Aaron Lande married Esther Boxim, March 1, 1854.
36. Harold Faulkner, *American Economic History,* p. 356.
37. *Nashville True Whig,* Jan. 21, 1854.
38. *Republican Banner* (Nashville), May 12, 1857.
39. *Nashville Daily Gazette,* Jan. 16, 1861; Jan. 19, 1861; Oct. 26, 1859.
40. Lillian Foster, *Wayside Glimpses,* p. 181.
41. Hon. Amelia M. Murray, *Letters from United States, Cuba and Canada,* Vol. II, p. 169; Henry McRaven, *Nashville Athens of the South,* pp. 82-83; *Nashville City and Business Directory* 1860-1869, pp. 32-38; Frederick Law Olmsted, *A Journey Through Texas; or a Saddle Trip on the Southwestern Frontier,* p. 36.
42. *Nashville Patriot,* Mar. 10, 1857.
43. William E. Dodd, *Expansion and Conflict,* p. 208.
44. W. W. Clayton, *History of Davidson County,* p. 208.

45. Foster, *op. cit.*, p. 188; Olmsted, *op. cit.*, p. 35.
46. Gower and Allen, *op. cit.*, p. 430. A Negro boy carried around a funeral notice written on a sheet of paper with a piece of crepe attached to the top and he handed this to passerbys to read; Edgar W. Martin, *The Standard of Living* in 1860, p. 247. Visitors from abroad interested in funeral processions attended by marching men from lodges, military and fire companies.
47. U.S. Bureau of the Census, *Population Schedule Free Inhabitants,* 1860, Isaac Stein reported ownership of real estate valued at $6000 and personal property at $23,000.
48. *Orr Collection,* manuscript section, Tennessee State Library and Archives. A bill to John Thompson from Nashville Furniture Mfg. Co., date Jan. 4, 1853 had following prices: mahogany bedstead $125, bureau $75, wardrobe $60, canopy $20, sewing chair $8.
49. *Nashville Union and American,* Mar. 9, 1854.
50. *Nashville Patriot,* Feb. 6, 1857; May 31, 1857; Apr. 17, 1859.
51. Ira P. Jones, *City of Nashville,* p. 100.
52. *Nashville Daily Gazette,* Jan. 16, 1861.
53. *Republican Banner* (Nashville), June 18, 1856.
54. Ella Lonn, *Salt as a Factor in the Confederacy,* p. 17.
55. Kathleen Ann Smallzreid, *The Everlasting Pleasure,* p. 134.
56. *Nashville Patriot,* June 16, 1858.
57. *Nashville Daily Gazette,* Sept. 7, 1854.
58. *Ibid.,* Jan. 1, 1861.
59. Matilda Livingston Rogers, *Recipe Book,* p. 68. A safe and sure emetic was drinking of one teaspoon of castor mustard mixed in a tumbler full of water; Eliza Leslie, *Miss Leslie's New Cook Book,* p. 612. Eggs may be preserved for a few months by putting in boiling water for one minute, then grease all over with melted fat and wedge down close together small end downward in a box of powdered charcoal; Smallzreid, *op. cit.,* p. 100. The cook is advised to put herself in order first . . . covering for hair, clean hands and nails, sleeves rolled up and clean apron.
60. Smallzreid, *op. cit.,* p. 99.
61. James Edward Alexander, *Transatlantic Sketches,* p. 269.
62. George Winfred Hervey, *The Principles of Courtesy,* p. 219.
63. *Republican Banner* (Nashville), Apr. 19, 1860.
64. *Nashville Daily Gazette,* Aug. 1, 1860.
65. *Ibid.,* Sept. 26, 1854.
66. *Nashville Union and American,* Feb. 18, 1855.
67. *Nashville Union and American,* June 15, 1855; *Nashville Patriot,* Sept. 7, 1860.

68. *Ibid.*
69. *Nashville Daily Gazette,* Feb. 17, 1857.
70. W. E. Baxter, *America and Americans,* p. 91; C. G. Rosenberg, *Jenny Lind in America,* p. 190. This author wrote, "there is more female loveliness in Nashville than you will find in any other city"; Rev. J. H. Ingraham, *Life and Experience of a Northern Governess in the Sunny South,* p. 72; Carlton H. Rogers, *Incidents of Travel in Southern States and Cuba,* p. 273.
71. I. J. Benjamin, *Three Years in America,* 1859-1862, trans. Chas. Reznikoff, Vol. I, pp. 89-91.
72. James D. Burn, "An English Workingman Takes a Dim View of American Women," *America in Perspective,* ed., Henry Steele Commager, p. 187.
73. *Harper's Monthly,* Vol. XIII, 1856, p. 78.
74. *Nashville Daily News,* May 27, 1858.
75. *Harper's Weekly,* Feb. 7, 1857.
76. *Ibid.,* Aug. 1, 1857, p. 487; *Nashville Daily Gazette,* July 26. 1860.
77. *Nashville Union and American,* Feb. 25, 1855.
78. *Nashville Daily Gazette,* Jan. 1, 1861.
79. Col. John Amenas Fite, "Memoirs," *Confederate Collection,* manuscript section, Tennessee State Library and Archives, p. 31.
80. *Harper's Weekly,* Aug. 4, 1860.
81. *Nashville Patriot,* Jan. 22, 1857.
82. *Ibid.,* July 23, 1858.
83. Foster, *op. cit.,* p. 158; *Octavia Zollicoffer Bond Papers,* manuscript section, Tennessee State Library and Archives. In a letter to Mrs. John Trotwood Moore, Mrs. Bond recalled that she lived with her parents in the City Hotel until she was six years of age; Edward Dicey, "Six months in the Federal States," *American Social History as Recorded by British Travelers,* ed., Allen Nevin, Vol. II, p. 397. Mr. Dicey was in Nashville in 1862 and had this to say about the hotel, "It was crammed with guests . . . was dirty . . . poorly managed . . . meals greasy due to white help disdainful of job and Negroes not working unless forced."; Emilie Marguerite Cowell, *The Cowells in America,* ed. M. Willson Disher, p. 100. Mrs. Cowell commented on dull hotel life bounded by eating, drinking, lounging about, staring at guests and occasionally playing the piano.
84. *Nashville Patriot,* June 3, 1858.
85. U.S. Bureau of the Census, *Statistics of the United States (including mortality, property, etc.)* in 1860, p. 512.
86. *Ibid.*
87. U.S. Bureau of the Census, *Population Schedule of Free Inhabi-*

tants, 1860. The 15 servants and employers were Bridget Mulgary, age 31, born Ireland, employer Lewis Solomon; Judy Regan, age 24, born Ireland, employer Henry Cohen; Anna Cornia, age 15, born Ireland, employer Sinai Nathan; Ella Murphy, age 25, born Ireland, employer I. M. Sobel; Ellen Flanegan, age 15, born Ireland, employer Louis Bloomstein; Catherine ? , age 43, born Ireland, employer Aaron Lande; ? ? , age 20, born Ireland, employer Henry Harris Boarding House; ? ? , age 14, born Ireland, employer Henry Harris Boarding House; Mary McCondree, age 40, born Scotland, employer David Elsbach; Theresa Rosen, age 18, born Poland, employer Myer Lusky; Margaret Buss, age 29, born Prussia, employer Isaac Stein; Mary Cook, age 17, born New York, employer S. Shyer; Mary Conrad, age 17, born New York, employer S. Laufer; Bettie Estes, age 9, born Virginia, employer Samuel Levick; Mary ? , age 9 (Mulatto), employer Jacob Ellis.

88. See note 27 in Chapter V for owners of slaves.
89. *Nashville Journal of Medicine and Surgery,* April 1851, Vol. I, No. 2, p. 126.
90. Daniel F. Wright (ed.), "Abstract of Proceedings of Nashville Medical Society at September Meeting," *The Nashville Monthly* 1859, pp. 101-102.
91. *The Temple Burial Book,* pp. 401, 402. Deaths are recorded for Barbara Stein, May 29, 1854; Lab Nassauer, Oct. 15, 1857; Joseph Stein, May 9, 1858; Jacob Mitchell, — 1859; Matilda Harris, July 10, 1859; S.K. (or S.H. or S.R.) Coleman, Sept. 19, 1859; Vogele (Phoebe) Heilbon, — 1860; Emil Heinefeilman, Mar. 30, 1860; Rebecca Elsbach, June 28, 1860; Esther Lande, Jan. 9, 1861; Marx Cline, Aug. 21, 1861. There are several unmarked graves listed, one of which may have been for Mrs. Isaac Garritson, Mar. 1856.
92. U.S. Bureau of the Census, *Population of United States in 1860,* p. XLIX.
93. *Nashville Daily Gazette,* Mar. 30, 1855.
94. *Harper's Monthly,* Vol. XIII, 1856, p. 76.
95. *Republican Banner* (Nashville), July 2, 1860.
96. *Nashville Daily Gazette,* May 2, 1861.
97. Cowell, *op. cit.,* p. 89. Mrs. Cowell remarked that she could not sleep because of bed-bugs.
98. Baxter, *op. cit.,* p. 91; Charles Dickens, *American Notes,* p. 170.
99. Francis Garvin Davenport, *Cultural Life in Nashville 1850-1860,* p. 78.
100. *Ibid.,* p. 57.
101. *Nashville Daily Gazette,* Mar. 29, 1851; Jan. 11, 1855; *Nashville*

Daily American, Dec. 23, 1851; *Republican Banner* (Nashville), Sept. 20, 1857; Feb. 7, 1860.

102. Foster, *op. cit.*, pp. 180-181. Miss Foster said drainage of streets was bad and added "Nashville is old fogey." Dicey, *op. cit.*, p. 397. Mr. Dicey wrote that Nashville was one of the cleanest and brightest towns at a distance but when one came close, the illusion vanished. Position of town made drainage easy, water abundant, only thing wanting was energy to keep place clean.

103. *Nashville, Board of Aldermen Minute Book*, 1857-1860, p. 269.

104. McGavock, *op. cit.*, p. 15.

105. *Republican Banner* (Nashville), May 21, 1857.

106. *Davidson County Criminal Court Minutes*, Book D, 1850-1854, p. 424. A. B. Oppenheimer a merchant was fined June 13, 1853 for assault with a pistol on Marcus Laski. *Ibid.*, Book E, 1854-1857, Louis Powers charged with assault and battery.

107. *Republican Banner* (Nashville), May 4, 1860.

108. U.S., Bureau of the census, *Population of United States in 1860*, pp. 456-457.

109. *Nashville Daily Gazette*, Oct. 22, 1857; *Nashville Union and American*, Apr. 18, 1860.

110. *Nashville Daily Gazette*, Oct. 22, 1857.

111. *Harper's Weekly*, Dec. 22, 1860.

112. *Nashville Daily Gazette*, Sept. 12, 1855; Oct. 22, 1857; *Nashville Union and American*, Apr. 18, 1860. Boys were suspected of setting fire to houses.

113. *Nashville Patriot*, Aug. 31, 1860; *Nashville Union and American*, Feb. 13, 1860.

114. *Nashville Patriot*, Feb. 4, 1857. Frederika Bremer, *America of the Fifties: Letters of Frederika Bremer*, p. 130.

115. *Bond Papers*—letter to Mrs. J. T. Moore, July 30, 1924.

116. *Ibid.*, Letter to Mrs. J. T. Moore, Jan. 28, 1932.

117. *Ibid.*

118. *Ibid.*, Letter to J. T. Moore, July 20, 1924.

119. *Nashville Patriot*, July 6, 1860.

120. A sampler made by Dorothy Hollstein Sulzbacher stamped 1831 is still in Sulzbacher family.

Bibliography

MANUSCRIPT MATERIAL

The Temple (Congregation Ohabai Sholom). Burial Book, 1854-1954.

Tennessee State Library and Archives. Octavia Zollicoffer Bond Papers.

Tennessee State Library and Archives. Confederate Collection.

Tennessee State Library and Archives. Foster Family Papers.

Tennessee State Library and Archives. The J. Emerick Nagy Collection.

Tennessee State Library and Archives. Orr Collection.

Tennessee State Library and Archives. Kenneth Daniel Rose Papers.

New York City Public Library. Matilda Livingston Rogers Recipe Book.

American Jewish Archives. (Photostat) Vital Records of Congregation Shearith Israel of New York.

LETTERS AND FAMILY RECORDS

Abrahams, Rolland. Letter to author, July 18, 1958.

Garritson, Isaac. Letter to Isaac Leeser, August 8, 1852.

Levy and Nassauer Family Records. Interview with Mrs. Emanuel Oury, Nashville, Tennessee.

Redelsheimer Family Records. Interview with Mrs. Stanley Simm of Nashville, Tennessee and Letter to author from Dr. Arthur C. Redelshumer of California.

Rosenfeld, Rabbi Alb. Letter to M. Elsbach, March 27, 1862.

Stern, Rabbi Malcolm H. Letters to author, September 25, 1958; October 8, 1958.

Sulzbacher-Spitz Family Records. Interviews with Mesdames Maurice Lowenthal and Sigmund Marks of Nashville, Tennessee.

DIRECTORIES, NEWSPAPERS, PERIODICALS

Nashville City and Business Directories. 5 vols. Publishers vary, 1853-1860-61.

Harper's Monthly. 1856.

Harper's Weekly. 1857; 1860.

Nashville Daily American. 1850; 1851; 1852; 1857.

Nashville Daily Gazette. 1849-1866.

Nashville Daily News. 1858; 1859.

Nashville Daily Union. 1847; 1848; 1854.

Nashville Patriot. 1856-1860.

Nashville Union and American. 1854-1860; 1875.

Nashville Whig. 1842; 1845; 1849; 1851; 1854.

National Banner and Nashville Whig. 1828.

Republican Banner (Nashville). 1841; 1842; 1852-1861; 1874.

The Asmonean. New York, 1849-1858.

The Israelite, Cincinnati, 1854-1862.

The Jewish Messenger. New York, 1857-1862.

The Occident and American Jewish Advocate. Philadelphia, 1843-1862.

PUBLIC DOCUMENTS

Davidson County. Chancery Court Minutes. 1854-1866.

_____. Circuit Court Minutes. 1838-1870.

_____. Criminal Court Minutes. 1845-1865.

_____. Deeds to Property. 1790-1870.

_____. Marriage Records. 1850-1865.

_____. Wills and Inventories. 1850-1865.

Nashville. Board of Aldermen Minutes. 1854-1860.

_____. *Revised Laws of City of Nashville.* 1806-1855.

New York City. Bureau of Municipal Archives and Records. 1854.

North Carolina. Secretary of State. *Abstract of North Carolina Wills.* By J. Bryan Grimes. Published under authority of the Trustees of the Public Libraries. Raleigh: E. M. Uzzell & Co. State Printers and Binders, 1910.

_____. *The State Records of North Carolina.* Edited by Walter Clark. 26 vols. Published under supervision of the Trustees of the public libraries, by order of the General Assembly. Goldsboro, N.C.: Nash brothers printers, 1886-1907.

Tennessee, Laws, Statutes, etc. *Acts of General Assembly.* 1848-1880.

U. S. Bureau of the Census. Population Schedule Free Inhabitants 1850; 1860.

_____. Population Schedule Slave Inhabitants. 1860.

_____. Population Schedule Inhabitants. 1870; 1880.

_____. *Report of the Superintendent of the Seventh Census.* Washington, 1853.

_____. *Statistical View of the U.S.—Being a Compendium of the Seventh Census.* Washington, 1854.

_____. *Preliminary Report of the Eighth Census.* Washington, 1862.

_____. *Population of the U.S. in 1860.* Washington, 1864.

——————. *Statistics of the U.S. (including Mortality, Property, etc.) in 1860.* Washington 1866.

——————. *A century of Population Growth from First Census to Twelfth 1790-1900.* Washington, 1909.

U. S. Congress, Senate. *Report of the Select Committee of the Senate of the United States on the Sickness and Mortality on Board Emigrant Ships.* Washington, 1854.

BOOKS, ARTICLES AND PAMPHLETS

Alexander, Sir James Edward. *Transatlantic Sketches*. London: R. Bentley, 1833.

Ambler, Charles Henry. *A History of Transportation in the Ohio Valley*. Glendale, Calif.: The Arthur H. Clark Company, 1932.

American Jews' Annual for 5646. Cincinnati: Leo Wise & Co., 1890.

Anderson, Douglas. "Negro Slavery and the White Man's Genius," *Nashville American*, October 16, 1904.

An Immigrant of One Hundred Years Ago: A Story of Someone's Ancestor, translated and retold by an old Hand. Hattiesburg: The Book Farm, 1941.

Bacon, Hollis Phillip II. "Historical Geography of Antebellum Nashville." Unpublished Ed. D. dissertation, George Peabody College for Teachers, 1955.

Baxter, W. E. *America and Americans*. London: G. Routledge & Co., 1855.

Belissary, Constantine. "The Rise of the Industrial Spirit in Tennessee 1865-1885." Unpublished Ph. D. dissertation, Vanderbilt University, 1949.

―――――――――. "Tennessee and Immigration 1865-1880," *Tennessee Historical Quarterly*, Vol. VII, No. 3, p. 230, Sept. 1948.

Bender, Eric. *Tickets to Fortune*. New York: Modern Age Books, 1938.

Benjamin, Isaac Joseph. *Three Years in America 1859-1862*. Translated by Charles Reznikoff. 2 vols. Philadelphia: Jewish Publication Society of America, 1956.

Bishop, A. L. and Keller, A. G. *Industry and Trade, Historical and Descriptive Account of their Development in the United States*. Boston: Ginn & Co., 1918.

Bowling, W. K. *An Oration Pronounced Upon the Occasion of the Laying of the Cornerstone of the Nashville High School*. Nashville: J. T. S. Fall, 1853.

Bransford, S. W. "A Letter to the Editor," *Nashville Banner*, November 18, 1931.

Bremer, Frederika. *America of the Fifties: Letters of Frederika Bremer*. Edited by Adolph B. Benson. New York: The American-Scandinavian Foundation, etc., 1924.

Burn, James D. "An English Workingman Takes a Dim View of American Women," *America in Perspective*. Edited by Henry Steele Commanger. New York: Random House, 1947.

Campbell, Mary E. R. "Tennessee and the Union 1847-1861." Unpublished Ph. D. dissertation, Vanderbilt University, 1937.

Cassedy, Ben. *History of Louisville*. Louisville: Hull and Brother, 1852.

Chambers, Wm. *Things as They are in America.* London: William and Robert Chambers, 1854.

Clark, Thos. D. "The Antebellum South 1825-1860," *Travels in the Old South, a Bibliography.* 3 vols. Norman: University of Oklahoma Press, 1959.

Clayton, W. W. *History of Davidson County.* Philadelphia: J. W. Lewis & Co., 1880.

Collins, S. H. *Emigrant's Guide to and Description of the United States of America.* London: Hull J. Noble, 1830.

Cooke, John C. "Memories of Days of Long Ago Recalled," *Nashville Banner,* September 6, 1931.

Cowell, Mrs. Emilie Marguerite. *The Cowells in America, Being the Diary of Mrs. Sam Cowell.* Edited by M. Willson Disher. London: Oxford University Press, 1934.

Darbey, Wm. *Emigrant's Guide.* New York: Kirk & Mercein, 1818.

Daughters of American Revolution (ed.). *The American Monthly Magazine,* Vol. II, Washington, 1854.

Davenport, Francis Garvin. "Cultural Life in Nashville 1850-1860." Unpublished Ph.D. dissertation, Vanderbilt University, 1936.

Dicey, Edward. "Six months in the Federal States," *American Social History as Recorded by British Travellers.* Edited by Allen Nevins. 2 vols. New York: H. Holt and Company, 1923.

Dickens, Chas. *American Notes.* New York: Harper & Brothers, 1842.

Dictionary of American Biography. 22 vols. New York: C. Scribner's Sons, 1928-36.

Dodd, William E. *Expansion and Conflict.* Boston: Houghton Mifflin Company, 1915.

Enelow, H. "Influence of Judaism in the South," *History of Social Life of the Southern States.* Vol. X of The South in the Building of the Nation. 13 vols. Richmond: The Southern Historical Publication Society, 1909.

Ernst, Robert. *Immigrant Life in New York City 1825-1863.* New York: King's Crown Press, 1949.

"Excerpts from the Scrap Books of Rev. J. J. Lyons," *Publications of the American Jewish Historical Society.* Vol. XXVII, 1920.

Excursion of the Fourth Day of July 1860—84th Anniversary of Declaration of Independence, a Heroic Poem in 9. Cantos. Nashville: John T. S. Fall, 1860.

Faulkner, Harold Underwood. *American Economic History.* New York: Harper and Bros., 1924.

First American Bank. *Firsts in Nashville, a Pictorial History.* [Nashville 1951].

First Annual Exhibition of the Mechanics Institute of Tennessee. Nashville: John F. Morgan, 1855.

169

Folmsbee, Stanley John. *Sectionalism and Internal Improvement in Tennessee, 1796-1845*. Knoxville: Stanley John Folmsbee, 1939.

Foner, Philip Sheldon. *Business and Slavery; the New York Merchants and the Irrepressible conflict*. Chapel Hill: The University of North Carolina Press, 1941.

Foster, Lillian. *Wayside Glimpses*. New York: Rudd & Carleton, 1860.

Frankland, A. E. "Fragments of History," *American Jews' Annual, 5650-51*. Cincinnati: Leo Wise & Co., 1890.

Friedman, Lee. *Jewish Pioneers and Patriots*. Philadelphia: The Jewish Publication Society of America, 1948.

_____. *Pilgrims in a New Land*. New York: The Jewish Publication Society of America, 1943.

Gohrman, Mary de. *Political Nativism in Tennessee to 1860*. Washington: The Catholic University of America, 1938.

Goodman, Abram V. "A Jewish Peddler's Diary in America," *American Jewish Archives*, Vol. III, No. 3, Cincinnati, 1951.

Gotthiel, Gustav, "The Position of the Jew in North America," *North American Review*, Vol. XXVI, Mar -Apr, 1878.

Gower, Hershel and Allen, Jack (ed.). *Pen and Sword, The Life and Journal of Randal W. McGavock*. Nashville: Tennessee Historical Commission, 1959.

Gray, Lewis Cecil. *History of Agriculture in the Southern United States to 1860*. 2 vols. Washington: The Carnegie Institution of Washington, 1933.

Grinstein, Hyman B. *The Rise of the Jewish Community of New York 1654-1860*. Philadelphia: The Jewish Publication Society of America, 1945.

Guild, Joseph Conn. *Old Times in Tennessee*. Nashville: Tavel, Eastman and Howell, 1878.

Hahn, Phyllis Elizabeth. "German Settlers in Nashville, Tennessee." Unpublished Master's dissertation, Vanderbilt University, 1935.

Hamer, Philip M. (ed.) *Tennessee: A History*. 4 vols. New York: The American Historical Society, Inc., 1933.

Handlin, Oscar. *Adventure in Freedom, Three Hundred Years of Jewish Life*. New York: McGraw-Hill Book Co., Inc., 1954.

_____. *The Uprooted*. Boston: Little Brown, 1951.

Hansen, Marcus. *The Atlantic Migration 1607-1860*. Cambridge: Harvard University Press, 1940.

_____. *The Immigrant in American History*. Cambridge: Harvard University Press, 1940.

Hargis, Robert Loren. "The Know Nothing Party in Tennessee." Unpublished Master's dissertation, Vanderbilt University, 1931.

Hawkins, R. C. "Old Resident Describes Nashville Business Section of Civil War Days," *Nashville Banner*, May 20, 1928.

170

Heller, James G. *As Yesterday When it is Past.* Cincinnati; Isaac M. Wise Temple, 1942.

Hervey, George Winfred. *The Principles of Courtesy.* New York: Harper & Brothers, 1852.

Hirshler, Eric E. *Jews from Germany in the United States.* New York: Farrar, Straus and Cudahy, 1955.

Hubbard, G. W. *A History of the Colored Schools of Nashville, Tennessee.* Nashville: Wheeler, Marshall & Bruce, 1874.

Huddleston, Ed. Nashville Its [sic] Personality and Progress [Nashville 1956].

Hume, Alfred. *Report on the Subject of Public Schools in the City of Nashville made to the Board of Mayor and Aldermen.* Nashville: W. F. Bang & Co., 1852.

Hunt, Freeman. *Worth and Wealth, Collection of Maxims and Morals for Merchants and Men of Business.* New York: Stringer & Townsend, 1856.

Hyamson, Albert M. *The Sephardim of England.* London: Metheun, 1951.

Illowy, Bernard. *Safer Milchamot Elohin: Being the Controversial Letters and the Casuistic Decisions of the Late Rabbi Bernard Illowy, Ph.D.* with a short history of his life and activities by his son Henry Illoway. Berlin: M. Poppelauer, 1914.

Ingraham, J. H. *Life and Experiences of a Northern Governess in the Sunny South.* New York: G. W. Carleton and Co., 1880.

Jewish Encyclopedia, The. 12 vols. New York: Funk & Wagnalls Company, 1901-1906.

Johnson, Gerald W. *An Honorable Titan.* New York: Harper & Brothers, 1946.

Jones, Ira P. *City of Nashville.* [Nashville 1890].

Jones, Ruth Irene. "Hot Springs: Ante bellum Watering Place," *Arkansas Historical Quarterly,* Vol. XIV, 1955.

Kisch, Guido. "A Voyage to America Ninety Years Ago," *Publications of the American Jewish Historical Society,* Vol. XXXV, 1939.

_____. *In Search of Freedom, a History of American Jews from Czechoslovakia.* New York: Block Publishing Co., 1949.

Knight, Edgar W. *Public Education in the South.* Boston; Ginn and Company, 1922.

Korber, Adolph. "Jewish Immigration from Württemberg to the United States 1848-1855," *Publications of the American Jewish Historical Society,* Vol. XLI, 1952.

Korn, Bertram W. *American Jewry and the Civil War.* Philadelphia: The Jewish Publication Society of America, 1951.

_____. *Eventful Years and Experiences.* Cincinnati: The American Jewish Archives, 1954.

Kouvenhoven, John A. *Adventures in America, a Pictorial Record from Harper's Weekly.* New York: Harper & Brothers, 1938.

Kraus, Michael. *The United States to 1865.* Ann Arbor: University of Michigan Press, 1959.

Leslie, Eliza. *Miss Leslie's New Cookery Book.* Philadelphia: T. B. Peterson, 1857.

Lewis, Liston. "Things Theatric in Nashville," *Nashville Banner,* Nov. 26, 1933.

Lieber, Francis. *The Stranger in America.* Philadelphia: Carey, Lea and Blanchard, 1835.

Lonn, Ella. *Salt as a Factor in the Confederacy.* New York: W. Neale, 1933.

McGavock, Randal W. *Communication from His Honor the Mayor transmitted to the City Council of Nashville, Tennessee, September 30, 1859.* Nashville: A. S. Camp, Patriot Job Rooms, 1859.

MacPherson, Joseph Tant Jr. "Nashville's German Element 1850-1870." Unpublished Master's dissertation, Vanderbilt University, 1957.

McRaven, Henry. *Nashville Athens of the South.* Chapel Hill: Tennessee Book Co., 1949.

Marcus, Jacob R. *Early American Jewry.* 2 vols. Philadelphia: The Jewish Publication Society of America, 1951-1953.

Martin, Edgar W. *The Standard of Living in 1860.* Chicago: The University of Chicago Press, 1942.

Meyer, B. Henry. *History of Transportation in the United States before 1860.* Washington: Carnegie Institution of Washington, 1917.

Michaux, F. A. *Travels to the Westward of the Allegheny Mountains.* London: Reprint from London edition, 1805.

Mulkey, William. *The Orthographical Spelling Book.* Nashville: Published for the author, 1856.

Murdoch, James E. *The Stage or Recollections of Actors and Acting.* Philadelphia: J. M. Stoddart & Co., 1880.

Murray, Hon. Amelia M. *Letters from United States, Cuba and Canada.* 2 vols. London: J. W. Parker & Son, 1856.

Nashville Board of Education. *First Report of the Board of Education and the Superintendent of Schools of Nashville.* Nashville, 1855.
——————. *Third Report of the Board of Education and the Superintendent of Schools of Nashville.* Nashville, 1857.
——————. *Rules for the Government of the Free Schools of the City of Nashville.* Nashville, 1855.

Nashville Journal of Medicine and Surgery. Vol. 1, No. 2. April, 1851.

Nashville, University of. *Catalogue of University of Nashville.* Nashville, 1859-1860.

Olmsted, Frederick Law. *A Journey Through Texas; or a Saddle Trip on the Southwestern Frontier.* New York: Dix, Edwards & Co., 1857.

Paxson, Francis L. "The Rise of Sports," *The Mississippi Valley Historical Review,* Vol. IV, No. 2, September, 1917.

Phillipson, David. "Jewish Pioneers of Ohio Valley," *Publications of the American Historical Society,* Vol. VIII, 1900.

Poor, Henry V. *Manual of the Railroads of the United States.* New York: Poor's Manual Company, 1869.

Rhodes, James Ford. *History of the United States from the Compromise of 1850.* 9 vols. New York: The McMillan Co., 1928.

Robertson Association. *Constitution of Robertson Association of City of Nashville.* Nashville: W. F. Bang & Co., 1856.

Rogers, Carlton H. *Incidents of Travel in Southern States and Cuba.* New York: R. Craighead, 1862.

Rosenberg, C. G. *Jenny Lind in America.* New York: Stringer & Townsend, 1851.

Sachar, Howard M. *The Course of Modern Jewish History.* Cleveland: World Publishing Company, 1958.

Schappes, Morris W. *A Documentary History of the Jews in the United States 1654-1874.* New York: The Citadel Press, 1950.

Simonhoff, Harry. *Jewish Notables in America, 1776-1865.* New York: Greenberg Publishers, 1956.

Smallzreid, Kathleen Ann. *The Everlasting Pleasure.* New York: Appleton-Century-Crofts, 1956.

Smith, Felix Randolph Robertson. *Alphabetical List of the Dead in the City Cemetery, Nashville, Tennessee, as shown by existing Monuments and Headstones.* [Nashville] 1909.

Steadman, E. *A Brief Treatise on Manufacture in the South.* Clarksville: C. O. Faxon, 1851.

Stephenson, George M. *A History of American Immigration 1820-1864.* Boston: Ginn & Co., 1926.

Tanner, H. S. *The View of the Valley of the Mississippi or the Emigrant's and Traveller's Guide to the West.* Philadelphia: Published by author, 1834.

Tennessee, Governors. *Messages of the Governors of Tennessee.* By Robert H. White, 5 vols. Nashville: Tennessee Historical Commission, 1952.

Todd, Herbert Henry. "The History of Education Legislation in Tennessee to 1860." Unpublished Master's dissertation, George Peabody College for Teachers, 1927.

Tryson, Warren S. "The Publications of Tichenor and Fields in the South 1840-1865," *The Journal of Southern History,* Vol. XIV, No. 3, August 1948.

Turest, David. "An appreciation of the Jewish Community in Nashville," *Nashville Y.M.H.A. News,* Dedication No. October 1924.

The Universal Jewish Encyclopedia. 10 vols. New York: The Universal Jewish Encyclopedia, Inc., 1939-1943.

Ward, Harold E. "Academy in Tennessee Prior to 1861." Unpublished Master's dissertation, George Peabody College for Teachers, 1926.

Watson, M. S. "Nashville During the Civil War." Unpublished Master's dissertation, Vanderbilt University, 1926.

Weeks, Stephen B. "Tennessee, a Discussion of the Sources of its Population," *Tennessee Historical Magazine,* Vol. II, December 1916.

Weidner, Maude. *Nashville Then and Now 1780-1930.* Nashville: Hermitage Publishing Company, 1930.

White, Robert Hiram. *Development of the Tennessee Educational Organization 1796-1929.* Kingsport: Southern Publishers, Inc., 1929.

Wiernik, Peter. *History of Jews in America.* New York: The Jewish Press Publishing Company, 1912.

Wilcox, Ruth Turner. *The Mode in Footwear.* New York: C. Scribner's Sons, 1948.

Williams, Samuel Cole. *Early Travels in the Tennessee Country 1540-1809.* Johnson City: The Watauga Press, 1928.

Wischnitzer, Mark. *To Dwell in Safety, a Story of Jewish Immigration Since 1800.* Philadelphia: The Jewish Publication Society of America, 1948.

Wittke, Carl. *Refugees of Revolution.* Philadelphia: University of Pennsylvania Press, 1952.

_____. *We, Who Built America, The Saga of the Immigrant.* New York: Prentice-Hall, Inc., 1940.

Woodring, T. V. *The City Cemetery of Nashville, Tennessee, facsimile of Original Records of Deaths and Burials.* Presented to the Tennessee Historical Society by the City of Nashville, 1955. Now in holdings of the Society at the Tennessee State Library and Archives.

Woods, Mary. *Memories and Recollections of Mary Woods.* [n.p. 1939].

Wright, Daniel F. (ed.) *The Nashville Monthly Record of Medical and Physical Science.* Nashville: A. S. Camp & Co., 1859.

Acknowledgments

I am indebted to the librarians and library staffs at the Nashville Public Library, the Tennessee State Library and Archives, the Hebrew Union College Library and Archives, the George Peabody College for Teachers, the Joint University Library and the Library of Congress for much valuable aid and assistance. Although it is not possible to name all persons who have been helpful, I wish to thank the following:

Dr. Jacob R. Marcus, Director of the American Jewish Archives at the Hebrew Union College–Jewish Institute of Religion, Cincinnati, Ohio, for his encouragement, advice, constructive criticism and prompt and courteous replies to innumerable letters over a seven year span of research; Mrs. Gertrude Parsley, of Tennessee State Library and Archives, for a critical reading of the entire manuscript and for assistance in the selection of illustrative material; Dr. Lou Silberman, of Vanderbilt University, for a critical review and advice on the first three chapters; Mr. Robert Quarles, retired archivist of Tennessee State Library and Archives, for reading and checking the first two chapters and for his valuable advice to use the 1850 census as a beginning point of research; Dr. Robert White, historian for State of Tennessee, for a critical reading of the chapter on education; Dr. Malcolm H. Stern, genealogist of the American Jewish Archives, for prompt, courteous and revealing replies to many questions relating to who's who in early American Jewry; Dr. Herbert Weaver, of Vanderbilt University, for an enlightening interview on local and Southern Jewish history; Mrs. Harriet Owsley for guidance in the use of manuscript material in the Tennessee State Library and Archives; Miss Kendall Cram for assistance in checking reference material; Mrs. Hermione Embry for genealogical information; Mr. Joseph Lutin for explanation of Garritson-Elsbach law suit; Mrs. Ben Pollack, Mrs. Jerome Small, Mrs. Morris Fishel, for assistance in proofreading; Mr. Rolland Abrahams and Mesdames Emanuel Oury, Sigmund Marks, Maurice Lowenthal, Allen Felknor and the late Mrs. Harry Joseph for interviews regarding family histories; Mrs. Stanley Simm for information on the Redelsheimer prayer book; Dr. Arthur Redelsheimer for a copy of the frontispiece of prayer book; Mrs. Myrtle Goodman for the gift of the Myer Lusky passport; Mrs. Charles Loventhal for the gift of the Alb Rosenfeld letter; Mrs. Leonard Werthan for the copy of picture of Lande children; Mrs. Jay Greenberg for copy of Sulzbacher sampler; Mr. Bernard Werthan, Sr. for copy of the Garritson letter; Mrs. Maurice Lowenthal for copies of the Spitz and Sulzbacher pictures; Mr. Forrest Reed and Mr. V. M. Whitesell for invaluable assistance in problems of publication.

And finally to my family who understandingly indulged a hobby that grew into this book.

Index

177

178